ST. MARY'S COLLEGE OF MARYLAND
ST. MARY'S CITY, MARYLAND 20686

Early America Revisited

Early America Revisited

Ivan Van Sertima

From the Library

of _____

Transaction Publishers

New Brunswick (U.S.A.) and London (U.K.)

Second Printing 1998
Copyright © 1998 Ivan Van Sertima

All rights reserved under International and Pan-American Copyright Conventions. No part of this book may be reproduced or transmitted in any form or by any means, electronic or mechanical, including photocopy, recording, or any information storage and retrieval system, without prior permission in writing from the publisher. All inquiries should be addressed to Transaction Publishers, Rutgers—The State University, 35 Berrue Circle, Piscataway, New Jersey, 08854-8042.

This book is printed on acid-free paper that meets the American National Standard for Permanence of Paper for Printed Library Materials.

Library of Congress Catalog Number: 98–13110
ISBN: 0–7658–0463–8
Printed in the United States of America

Library of Congress Cataloging-in-Publication Data

Van Sertima, Ivan.
    Early America revisited / Ivan Van Sertima.
       p.   cm.
    Includes bibliographical references.
    ISBN 0–7658–0463–8 (alk. paper)
    1. America—Discovery and exploration—African. 2. Africans—
America—History.   3. America—Antiquities.   4. Egypt—Antiquities.
I. Title.
E109.A35V35   1998
970.01'9—dc21   98–13110
                                                                CIP

Contents

Early America
Revisited

1

The Mandingo Voyages (A.D. 1310, 1311)

It is now twenty-one years since *They Came Before Columbus: The African Presence in Early America* was first published. It appeared from Random House in 1976 and is now in its twenty-first printing. Like most controversial works it has attracted the most extreme and vicious criticism as well as the most enthusiastic praise. Like most controversial works also, its most voluble commentators have either read it superficially or misread it, for it is often praised and attacked for the wrong reasons, for saying things I did not say, for advancing positions I would neither entertain nor defend.

In November 1991, I presented a clarification and update of my thesis in an address to the Smithsonian. This was published four years later by the Smithsonian Institution Press in a book entitled *Race, Discourse and Origin of the Americas* (edited by Rex Nettleford and Vera Hyatt.)[1] Recently, however, a trio of scholars, with two of whom I have previously clashed, and effectively thrashed (see chapter 4: Reply to My Critics) have banded together to misrepresent and discredit my work. It has therefore become necessary to present the evidence that has emerged since then in this expanding field, to clarify the stands I took two decades ago, to reexamine and present anew the case for pre-Columbian contacts between Africans and native Americans—the Mandingo voyages of A.D. 1310, 1311, the earlier Egypto-Nubian contact in the time of Ramses III (c. 1200 B.C.) as well as that of the Nubian dynastic era (the 25th dynasty) when we find a duplication of the unique ritual and ceremonial complex of their royal cousins of the north.

I had hoped, that when the time came for me to deal with my critics I would be dealing with serious and honest scholars who disagree with me on the basis of contrary and indisputable new evidence. My trio of critics (Bernard Ortiz de Montellano, Warren Barbour, and Gabriel Haslip-Viera) writing in an issue of *Current Anthropology* raise but one legitimate question and that is over the dating of the very first contact with outsiders from the African world. That dating relates to the era of Ramses III (c. 1200 B.C.) which precedes the era of the Nubians which I had first highlighted but, while the Nubian contact is later, it duplicates, with only one possible exception, the ritual and ceremonial complex of the north. Also, no Egyptian journey to "the far West of the World" at that time, would have excluded Nubians. Also, both the motive and capacity for the journey existed in both periods. I made it very clear in my address to the Smithsonian in 1991 that this contact was possible at both ends of the dating equation. My critics are well aware of this. One of them (Ortiz de Montellano) follows my every word, as a bloodhound follows the scent of his prey. My address was made as early as November 1, 1991, and it was circulated far and wide even before its publication by the Smithsonian Press in 1995. To pretend therefore that I had not made allowance for this, especially in my study of ritual correspondences and influences, is an act of gross dishonesty.

Almost every other objection to my thesis is generated by sheer revulsion at the suggestion that "*flat-nosed Negroes*"* could have developed an ancient civilization, could in any way be related to the "*long, narrow-nosed*"* Egyptians and Nubians.[2] Revulsion also at the thought that they could cross an ocean before the "discoverer", Christopher Columbus, a man blessed with expert geographical knowledge and navigational skills, so blessed indeed that he believed at first he had stumbled upon the backside of India, that Cuba was the continent, South America an island, and the Caribbean sea the Gulf of the Ganges.

I am grateful, however, in a way, that I have been provided with an opportunity, through this concerted attack, to *restate and update*, in the clearest possible manner, the case for an African presence in America, *before Columbus*, by Africans from the Mandingo empire of

---

*Quoted from my critics who claim that "none of the early Egyptians and Nubians looked like Negroes" ... "They have long narrow noses ... short, flat noses are confined to the West African ancestors of African-Americans" They will get quite a shock when they see photos of ancient Egyptians and Nubians in this book.

Mali as well as well as for an Egypto-Nubian presence in both Central and South America before the Christian era.

"The most important of these alleged voyages" says my trio of critics, *"was that of Abu Bakari II, the Mandingo emperor of Mali, in* A.D. *1311, but no artifact of African origin has ever been found in the New World."*[3]

I shall begin with evidence for these "alleged" voyages to America in the 14th and 15th centuries, evidence in more than a dozen categories. I shall also cite a pre-Columbian artifact of African origin found in the New World by European adventurers and explorers who accompanied Columbus as well as pre-Columbian African skeletons found in a grave in the Caribbean dated A.D. 1250, about two and a half centuries before Columbus.

As I pointed out to a Congressional Committee, overlooking the work of the Christopher Columbus Quincentenary Commission,[4] I am not the first person to suggest that there were Africans in America before Columbus. Christopher Columbus is the first person to suggest this. He was also the first to present hard incontestable proof of it. Columbus reported in his *Journal of the Second Voyage*—and this is quoted in many places, not just in his Journal—that when he was in Haiti (which the Spanish called Española) the native Americans told them that black-skinned people had come from the south and southeast in boats, trading in gold-tipped metal spears. It is recorded in *Raccolta, Parte 1, Volume 1*, (John Boyd Thacher, 1903)

> Columbus wanted to find out what the Indians of Española had told him, that there had come from the south and southeast, Negro people, who brought those spear points made of a metal which they call guanin, of which he had sent samples to the king and queen for assay which which was found to have 32 parts—18 of gold, 6 of silver and 8 of copper.[5]

Columbus actually sent samples of these spears back on a mail boat to Spain to be assayed. The proportion of gold, silver and copper alloys were found to be identical with spears being forged at that time in African Guinea. Apart from the eyewitness testimony of the native Americans, here is incontestable metallurgical evidence from Europeans themselves (their meticulous assays establishing the identical proportion of metal alloys in the spears found in the Caribbean and the spears made in Guinea). Not only that. The names for these gold-tipped spears offer us a series of identical sounds in both language areas. Among the Mandinga we have *ghana, kane, kani, kanine, ghanin.* In the pre-Columbian Caribbean we have *goana, caona, guani, guanin, guanini.*[6] Another word used to refer to gold in the pre-Columbian Caribbean and metal with gold alloys, was, as Las Casas reports, *nucay* or *nozay.* This is equally close in sound to the Mande nege (pronounced *nuh-GHAY*) and nexe (pronounced *nuh-KHUH*) which stands for any kind of metal ornament or jewelry.[7]

DIALECT	WORD	MEANING
Sarakole Soninké Gadsago	*kane*	gold
Vai Mende	*kani*	metal (gold/silver)
Kissi	kanie	gold
Kono	*kanine*	gold
Peul	kanne	gold

Diagram of gold words in West Africa corresponding to those used for the gold-tipped spears in America.

Columbus is joined by nearly a dozen Europeans who reported seeing or hearing of "Negroes" when they first came. One of these is Ferdinand. a son of Columbus, who wrote a book on his father, in which he states his father told him that he had seen "negroes" north of Honduras.[8] Several of the European visitors of the Columbus contact period reported seeing, or hearing of, black Africans among the native Americans during the first phase of the European contact period and they were certainly not seeing pre-visions of the slave blacks they were to bring into these territories later. They reported on these encounters in a manner that indicated their great surprise.

Vasco Nuñez de Balboa, on 25 September 1513, coming down the slopes of Quarequa, which is near Darien (now called Panama) saw two tall black men who had been captured by the native Americans. He and his party were so astonished that they questioned the natives closely about these strange blacks. And the natives said "we do not know where these people come from. All that we know is that they live in a large settlement nearby and are waging war with us."[9] Peter Martyr, reporting on this meeting, said that Negroes had been shipwrecked in that area and had taken refuge in the mountains. Martyr refers to them as "Ethiopian pirates".[10] The word "Ethiopian" as used in this context, does not refer to people from Ethiopia. It springs from "aethiops" which means "burnt skin". People of sun-burnt skin (that is, blacks) were sometimes referred to, at that point in time, in this broad and general way.

Lopez de Gomara also describes the blacks Europeans sighted for the first time in Panama: "These people are identical with the Negroes we have seen in Guinea." [11] De Bourbourg also reports that there were two peoples indigenous to Panama—the Mandinga (black skin) and the Tule (red skin)[12]. Why would all these Europeans provide sworn testimony to the presence of Africans in Panama if they had never been seen there? Africans were not strangers to the Spanish and Portuguese. Black Africans and Arabs had invaded Southern Europe in 711 A.D. and had established dynasties that profoundly affected Spain, Portugal and Sicily until the year 1492, the year the African general Boabdil of the Almohade dynasty surrendered (see photo) the very year Columbus set sail for the New World.[13]

Columbus also was very well aware of the African in other contexts. He was in Guinea at the court of the Portuguese king, Don Juan, ten years before 1492. Columbus not only heard of blacks in Haiti and saw them north of Honduras (according to what he told his son Ferdinand) but on one voyage he split his fleet (May 30, 1498) "to investigate the report of the Indians of Espanola who said there had come to Espanola from the south and southeast a black people who have the tops of their spears made of a metal which they call guanin."[14]

Michael Coe, although an opponent of my thesis, noted in a letter to one of my former students, Keith Jordan, that Alonzo Ponce reported blacks landing on the North American coast in pre-Spanish times. Ponce speaks of a boatload of "Moors", using the word as the Greeks and Romans used it (Greek *maures*, Roman *maurus*=black, dark) who landed off Campeche in pre-Columbian Mexico and "terrorized the natives."

Alphonse de Quatrefages, author of *The Human Species*, reports on distinct black tribes among the native American—black communities such as the Jamassi of Florida, the Charruas of Brazil, and a people in St Vincent. He presents a map drawn by a French sea-captain, Kerhallet, showing independent black settlements along the South American coasts where landfalls had been made by black Africans.[15]

There were other reports and sightings. Father Roman (Ramon Pane), one of the twelve missionaries to visit the Americas soon after Columbus' so-called discovery states that the African gold merchants who came to Hispaniola were called the Black Guanini.[16] Rafinesque asserts that "Guanini" implied " the Golden Tribe" and referred to black merchants who trafficked in gold.[17] Rodrigo de Colmenares, in his Memorial against Vasco Nuñez de Balboa, wrote that "a captain brought news of a black people located east of the Gulf of San Miguel—'i que habia alli cerca gente negra.[18] Also, Fray Gregoria Garcia reports on Blacks sighted off Cartagena, Columbia. "These are the first Negroes we have seen in the Indies."[19]

I have cited twelve *European* witnesses—Christopher Columbus, Ferdinand Columbus, Vasco Nunez de Balboa, Peter Martyr, Lopez de Gomara, Rodrigo de Colmenares, Captain Kerhallet, L'Abbé Brasseur de Bourbourg, Alonzo Ponce, Ramon Pane, Riva Palacio (see p. 154) and Gregoria Garcia. It would appear, according to my critics, that these people were only saying so because the transatlantic crossing had made them too dizzy to distinguish Africans from native Americans or because, although they were all European, they had come down with a mysterious twentieth-century disease, diagnosed as "Afrocentricity", an optical disease that so damaged their Eurocentric vision that everywhere they looked—whether it was in Panama or Haiti or Honduras or Cartagena, Columbia, or Campeche in Mexico or east of the Gulf of San Miguel or in Tegucigalpa, (on the Nicaraguan-Honduran border) or in Florida, Brazil or St. Vincent—they were seeing big black spots before their eyes that made them imagine they were actually seeing Africans far from their dens in the jungle, striking out in foreign places like real humans, when they had not yet properly taught them to think and speak intelligently, store food, build boats, venture beyond their primitive lair across unchartered spaces.

Apart from the eyewitness accounts of the Europeans who saw or heard of these people, I have cited metallurgical and linguistic evidence for such a contact (the gold-tipped spears with an identical ratio of gold, silver and copper alloys as spears found in African Guinea and a range of identical-sounding names associated with these spears). But there is also evidence found in nine other disciplines establishing pre-Columbian contact between Africa and America.

There is the botanical evidence which my critics seek to deny, claiming that I misquoted the authority, S.G. Stephens, on this matter. I will not summarize him in my words but quote him directly on this matter of a New World cotton being introduced into West Africa before 1492.

The botanist S.G. Stephens reports: "Attempts at settlement of the Cape Verde Islands quickly followed and by 1466 cottons from Guinea had been introduced and already become semiferal. Today, according to Teixera and Barbosa (1958) it occurs in a wild sub-spontaneous state in the arid areas of most of the islands. It is a New World cotton (*G. hirsutum var. punctatum*). It is clear that if the wild cottons of today are descendants of the cottons introduced from Guinea between 1462 and 1466, *then a New World cotton must have been established in Africa before Columbus's first voyage*.[20]

With respect to American zea mays in pre-Columbian Africa, let me quote Dr. David Kelley in his critical appraisal of the evidence I presented for this in our Smithsonian debate.

"The kind of evidence field archeologists like is the pavement of Île Ife, a former Yoruba capital (Van Sertima 1976:264–267). This is made from broken potsherds that were decorated by rolling corncobs over their surface before firing. Paul Mangelsdorf, who had seen some of the sherds assured me (about 1954) that they were indeed Zea mays. Another interpretation of Yoruba tradition is that the capital was moved from Île Ife to Old Oyo about A.D. 1100 or earlier (M.D.W. Jeffreys, 1953). If so, this site provides the hard evidence that archeologists want for American plants in Africa in pre–Columbian times."[21]

One of the major elements that has been completely ignored in the study of contacts between the Old World and the New in the medieval period is the fact that both North and West Africa were in positions of ascendancy at that point of time. Africans and Arabs had invaded Southern Europe and had established four dynasties which profoundly affected Spain, Portugal and Sicily. The first two dynasties (the Ummayad and Abbaside dynasties) were dominated by Arab elements, although there were African elements in the mix as well. The last two—the Almoravide and the Almohade—were dominated by Africans (*see photo of the African general Boabdil surrendering in Granada on January 2nd, 1492*, p.8, the very year Columbus set sail for the Americas).[22] Portuguese documents of the Moorish period clearly show that Africans had not only penetrated southern Europe but had ad-

African General Boabdil (Abu-Abdi-Llah) surrenders to the Spanish (Granada, 1492).

vanced west across the sea into another world. The holocaust that devastated Africa after 1492, reducing millions of blacks to the status of subhumans, has made all this seem at this point in time pure fantasy. But make no mistake. The evidence has not just disappeared. The Portuguese actually informed Columbus on Saturday evening, March 9, 1493, a week after he had been driven by a storm into Lisbon, following his first voyage to the Indies, that "boats had been found that started out from Guinea and navigated to the west with merchandise."[23]

The Portuguese weren't guessing about African boats starting out from Guinea and going far to the west with merchandise. A 1448 map, using the Cape Verde point of the Upper Guinea coast as a reference, actually shows the outlines of Brazil and calculates it as "1500 miles to the west".[24] I reproduce this pre-Columbian map (on the following page). It is the Andrea Biancho map. I was not even aware of it when I wrote *They Came Before Columbus*. Harold Lawrence, who, unlike me, concentrated wholly and solely on the Mandingo journeys (as did Leo Wiener) made me aware of this in 1986, ten years after I had completed my work. I take this opportunity to reproduce the map. It appears in the *Journal of African Civilizations* (vol. 8, no. 2), which I edited and published in 1986. It shows why the Portuguese were so sure that African boats had started out from Guinea and navigated to the west and why they were so anxious, now that Columbus had crossed the ocean under the flag of Spain, to draw a demarcation line 370 leagues west of the Cape Verde (roughly 1500 miles, according to Amerigo Vespucci) to prevent the rival power of Spain from moving in and asserting dominion over everything. That is why they intrigued with Columbus on Saturday evening, March 9, 1493, a week after he had been driven by a storm into Lisbon, following his first voyage to the New World.[25]

My critics claim that nothing African has been found in pre-Columbian America, not a single artifact. I have already pointed to the gold-tipped spears, to which, not only Columbus and the Portuguese, but even the metallurgists in Spain, give testimony. But there is also a find of African skeletons in a pre-Columbian New World grave. Two African skeletons were found in a grave dated A.D. 1250. (note the date: it is roughly $2^{1}/_{2}$ centuries before Columbus) at Hull Bay, St. Thomas, in the U.S. Virgin Islands. These skeletons, according to the Smithsonian, were of two African males in their thirties. Not only

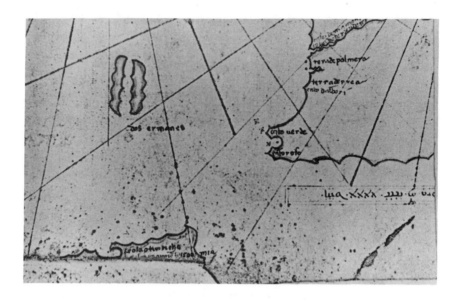

A portion of Andrea Biancho's Map of A.D. 1448. The inscription on the land mass represented in the lower left hand corner of the map reads "ixola otinticha xe longa aponente 1500 mia," which translates from the medaeval Italian into modern English as "Authentic island is distant 1500 miles to the west." This would be to the west of the Cape Verde point of the Upper Guinea coast. A tracing from an enlarged photograph of this "authentic island" gives a clearer representation of the inscription:

Although this land mass is drawn much closer to Cape Verde than Brazil actually is, the notation "1500 miles to the west" erases any doubts about its geographical position. The long stretch of coastline, drawn with great care, corresponds to the shape of the northeast corner of Brazil.

PANAMA	WEST AFRICA
Sierre de MALI 1)—A mountain range in Darien which corresponds to the general location where the Indians of Quareca told Balboa Blacks resided. 2)—This range lies east of the Gulf of San Miguel, approximately where one Of the Colmenares' captains reported the presence of Blacks.	MALI 1)—A vast West African empire whose center lay in the mountainous area at the headwaters of the Senegal/Niger. 2)—Niani, one of the famous Mandinga capitals, was also called by this name. 3)—A synonym for Mandinga.
MANDINGA 1)—A town of anchorage located on a Bay of the same name, both facing the Gulf of San Blas. 2)—A river following across Panama and emptying into the MANDINGA BAY. 3)—A black people who live among the Cuna Indians near San Blas.	MANDINGA 1)—The name of an extensive geographical region of West Africa, which was the nucleus of the Mali Empire. The name was often used as a synonym for Mali. 2)—One of the most numerous ethnic confederations in West Africa. They have diffused throughout much of that area.
CANA GUANA 1)—CANA was the name of a town where an important gold mine was worked. It was located on a river by the same name. 2)—GAUNA, also known as Chuana, was a black tribe which migrated south of Darien into the province of Chocó. They are believed to be the remnants of the Blacks seen by Balboa and Colmenares around 1513.	GHANA 1)—The name of an ancient West African empire and its capital city. It later became a province of Mali under Mandinga authority. 2)—A name for gold. 3)—The title of a king which meant "war leader" in Mandinga. 4)—The name of a people who were a significant element in the province of Ghana.
CARACOLE 1)—A pointe of land in southwest Panama.	CARAGOLE, CARAGOLI, SARAKOLE- 1)—A branch of the great Mandinga family. CARACOLE, or CARAGOLI, are the more ancient forms which were used as generic names for Mandinga.
BARBACOAS- BERBICE- 1)—BARBACOA is a town on the Chagres River. The name is also used to refer to a tribal/linguistic group scattered throughout Panama and extending southward into the southern regions of Colombia. 2)—A swampy lowland area in Panama.	BARBACUA BARBACIS BARBASINS- 1)—BARBACUA was the name of port town at the mouth of the Senegal. 2)—BARBACIS, or BARBASIN, was the generic name for the Serers who live in the general area of BARBACUA and who were ocean-going fishermen under the authority of Mandinga.

Mandinga place names found in Panama where Balboa and his men sighted "pre-slave trade" Africans.

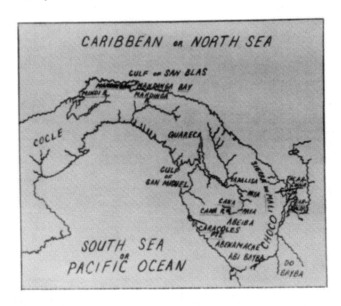

The Isthmus of Panama (Darien). Several important locations that relate to the pre-Columbian Mandinga presence in the area are noted. Most of these sites were outlined in Cullen's surveys for the Panama Canal and Railroad.

were they morphologically African but a peculiar dental ritual observed among certain Africans (filing of the incisor teeth) was reported. Moreover, a pre-Columbian native American ornament was found around the forearm of one of these skeletons. When, however, an attempt was made to carbon date them, the investigators found they could not. Something unusual had entered the area, affecting the dating of the bones. What it was cannot be disclosed at this point in time since it is "classified information". Fortunately, however, the matter does not end there. For, not far from where the African skeletons were found, a dot and crescent script of African origin was discovered (see illustration) It was found carved deeply in the rock face of an ancient waterfall at St. John's. It was deciphered by the Libyan Department of Antiquities. It is the Tifinagh branch of the Libyan script, which was once used not only by Southern Libyans but by the Tamahaq Berbers and a people in medieval Mali. It reads" "Plunge in to cleanse impurity. This is water for ablution before prayer."[26] (see photo p. 13)

What makes many scholars reject the possibility that early Africans could cross oceans is because they were trained, as I was, to concen-

B-B —K   K $\overset{W}{D}$ $\overset{K}{D}$ $\overset{W-S-\overset{\cdot}{A}}{D-\overset{\cdot}{A}-D}$ S-K $\overset{K-}{(=q)}$ $\overset{\overset{\cdot}{A}}{W}$ ←Start

Reading from right to left, in Libyan Arabic,

W-a-q K-s d-a-d a-s-w K-d w-d K —K-b-b, or, rendered in modern Arabic

وْ‌قٍ دَكْ دْو كْدٍ اسْول كْلَدْ رْسُ وٓقٍ‌دْ

"Plunge in to cleanse and dissolve away impurity and trouble; this
is water for ritual ablution before devotions".

Barry Fell's Decipherment

Dot and crescent formation on rock at bottom of the Reef Bay Valley, St.
John's. U.S. Virgin Islands. Verified as Tifinag branch of Libyan script
by Libyan Department of Antiquities.

trate on the study of the African primitive. The canoes that Tarzan turned over so easily in the movies seem still to be the working model in many minds of what the African had to offer in this regard. Let me therefore outline briefly the types of African boats that have been tested successfully on the world's oceans (in particular, the Atlantic) and the swiftly moving marine conveyor belts that take boats from the African to the American continent and back again. It is not only the layman that is at sea here. Few anthropologists have ever studied the pull and pace and power of vast bodies of water.

There are three major currents off the Atlantic coast of Africa that will carry a craft automatically, irresistibly, unless it has engines to break the almost magnetic pull of the water. One of these currents flows off the Cape Verde islands, another off the Senegambia coast, the third off the southern coast of Africa (see map of currents).

African boats of both ancient and medieval design have been tested on these currents and crossed the Atlantic successfully. Thor Heyerdahl, with the help of Buduma boatmen on Lake Chad, rebuilt a pre-Christian African craft—a papyrus reed boat—and crossed the Atlantic successfully. (see p. 16) Hannes Lindemann discovered that Africans had enormous dugouts as large as Viking ships. He tested one of these and made it to America in 52 days, 12 days less than Amerigo Vespucci, even though Vespucci left from an equally favorable starting point on the African-Atlantic coast (*They Came Before Columbus*, p. 62). Dr. Alain Bombard rode a liferaft from Casablanca in North Africa via the Canaries to Barbados in 1952 without stocking up with adequate supplies of food and water, with only a cloth net for small sea fauna, a fishing line with hook for tunny, and two spears. He also carried a container for collecting water when the rain fell. He survived in perfect health (*They Came Before Columbus*, p. 64).

African boatmen from Lake Chad built an ancient papyrus reed boat along the pattern of the ancient Egyptians. Thor Heyerdhal financed this experiment since he was aware that Africans were using these types of boats long before Christ. He bought twelve tons of payrus reed to carry out this experiment. Its success startled the world. Heyerdahl made one mistake. He had advised the Buduma to alter the ancient rudder. All seemed to go well until they neared Barbados when the RA listed and went into "drift mode". But this mistake merely slowed them down. The Buduma sailed into the New World on their ancient craft without assistance.

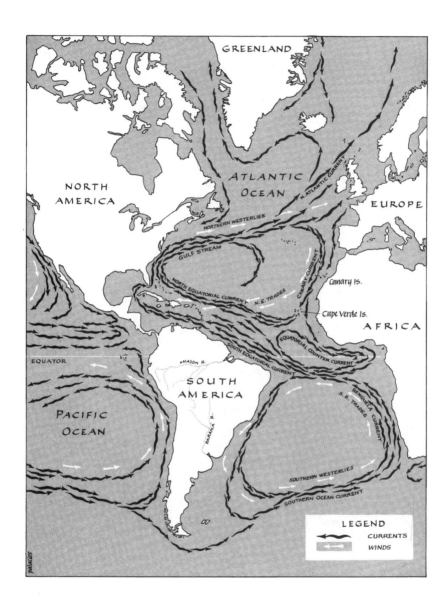

World-wide winds and currents, emphasizing Atlantic drift routes from Africa to America.

Heyerdahl's Ra I, built by African boatmen. African boatmen from Lake Chad built this papyrus boat along the pattern of the ancient Egyptians. It left North Africa in 1969 and sailed as far as Barbados.

The Africans also had trading ships that sailed the Indian Ocean between East Africa and China two centuries before Columbus set sail for the New World on the Santa Maria. I present a model of an East African trading ship of great antiquity. It sailed the Indian Ocean between Africa and China (see photo). Held together not by nails but by palm-fiber lashings, these ships could be as heavy as 70 tons. The one I show here is from a model in the Fort Jesus museum in Mombasa. The Swahili transhipped an elephant to China in the thirteenth century.

There is also the iconographic evidence, that is, evidence of the African image in paintings and sculptures of pre-Columbian Mexico. This for me was the most persuasive although the very last for me to discover. I had read the work of Leo Wiener. In fact, that was the only thing I read, and this by sheer accident, during a brief weekend in America twenty-seven years ago. I was only partly impressed. It could not shake the stubborn Eurocentric image I had had of the African, an

East African trading ship. A ship of great antiquity, it sailed the Indian Ocean between Africa and China. Held together not by nails but by palm-fiber lashings, these ships could be as large as 70 tons. The one shown here is from a model in the Fort Jesus museum at Mombasa. The Swahili transshipped an elephant to China in the thirteenth century.

image partially shattered by my actual experience in Africa and yet subconsciously consolidated by my colonial past and my British education. Wiener could not shake that. He presented some facts that startled me but his pictographic evidence was weak and failed to convince me. I was the first linguist to compile a *Swahili Dictionary of Legal Terms*, based on my field work in East Africa, and so I could appreciate some of the linguistic links he forged. But I came away from his work with such gnawing doubts that when I returned to live and teach in America a year later I actually began a systematic critique of his thesis. I sent this critique to the editor of a magazine—*Amistad*, vol. 2—which issue was never to see the light of day. I concluded my critique of Wiener with the words . . .,"If anyone can show me just one image of an African in America before Columbus, I would be willing to take another hard look at this matter." To my astonishment, the editor called me up a week later. "I've just looked at your piece," he said, "and a strange thing happened just after I read your conclusion. There, right before my eyes, were the kind of images you were looking for. The novelist John Williams (author of *The Man Who Cried I Am*) has just come back from Mexico. There he met a German professor, Alexander Von Wuthenau. He teaches art history at the University of the Americas. This German guy is a baron, by the way, last of the royal house of Germany. He gave John some photos that are practically shouting back at you. You've got to see them." When I did, I was so startled that I destroyed my critique. These were some stunning photos of pre-Columbian African sculptures in Mexico. I flew to San Angel the following weekend to meet this extraordinary man (see photo). That meeting was to transform my work, my vision, my life. It is equally strange that I was the last person to speak to him and to bring him joyful news of a joint triumph over our most formidable enemies just before he died.[28]

As I said in my introduction to *They Came Before Columbus*: "Professor Van Wuthenau had done extensive researches of private collections and museums in the Americas and also his own excavations in Mexico. A generation of work in this area had unearthed a large number of Negroid heads in clay, gold, copper and copal sculpted by pre-Columbian American artists. The strata on which these heads were found ranged from one of the early American civilizations right through to the edge of the Columbus contact period. Accidental stylization could not account for the individuality and racial particulars of these

Van Sertima meets Von Wuthenau. San Angel, Mexico.

heads. Their Negro-ness could not be explained away nor, in most cases, their African cultural origin. Their coloration, fullness of lip, prognathism, scarification, tattoo markings, beards, kinky hair, generously fleshed noses, and even, in some instances, identifiable coiffures, headkerchiefs, compound earrings—all these had been skillfully and realistically portrayed by pre-Columbian potters, jewelers and sculptors.

Terracotta sculpture of faces was the photography of the pre-Columbian Americans and what Von Wuthenau had done was to open new rooms in the photo gallery of our lost American ages. No longer was the African chapter in American pre–Columbian history an irrecoverable blank because of the vicious destruction of American books. Here were visible witnesses of a vanished time and they were telling us a new story."[29]

That story was also being told on the other side of the world. The oral tradition of medieval Mali speaks of an African king, Abu Bakari II, who sent two separate fleets comprising hundreds of boats across the Atlantic between 1310 and 1312. This history has not just been

Mandingo head in fourteenth-century Mexico. Made by the Mixtecs, from Oaxaca. Josue Saenz collection, Mexico City.

(a) Negroid head with vivid scarification (Vera Cruz, Classic Period)

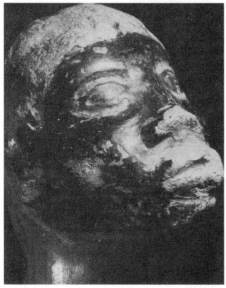

(b) Negroid head worshipped by Aztecs as *representation of* their god Tezcatlipoca because it had the right ceremonial color (Please note: This is *not* the god. It was seen as "a representation of" the god because its "literal blackness" evoked the "symbolic dark force" of Texcatlipoca.)

Plate 17 *Bearded Negroid wanderers in medieval Mexico*. **From the Mixtec Codex Dorenberg (fourteenth century). Note beards, lips, noses of these foreigners, who are represented with black skins. While pictorial representations here are not as photographically realistic as some of the terracotta portraitures, alien and distinctive features are emphasized.**

transmitted orally. It appears in Arabic documents—*Al-Qalqashandi* and *Masalik el Absar fir Mamelik el Amsar*.

When Mansa Musa, the most famous of the Mandinga emperors of Mali, stopped in Cairo on his way to Mecca in 1324, he reported that his brother, Abu Bakari II, who had preceded him, had launched two expeditions to discover the limits of the Atlantic. Al Umari, writing a few decades after Mansa Musa's visit, reports on these voyages.

"I asked the Sultan Musa," says Ibn Amir Hajib, "how it was that power came into his hands." "We are," he told me, "from a house that transmits power by heritage. The ruler who preceded me would not believe that it was impossible to discover the limits of the neighbouring sea; he wanted to find out and persisted in his plan. He had two hundred ships equipped and filled them with men, and others in the same number filled with gold, water and supplies in sufficient quantity to last for years. He told those who commanded them "return only when you have reached the extremity of the ocean or when you have exhausted your food and water." They went away; their absence was long before any of them returned. Finally, a sole ship reappeared. We asked the captain about their adventures.

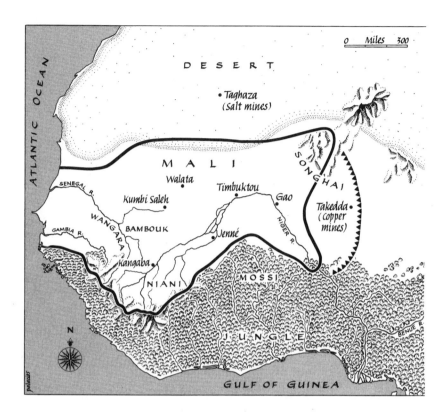

Medieval Mali at the time of Abubakari the Second. Its physical dimensions dwarfed the Holy Roman Empire.

"Prince," he replied, "we sailed for a long time, up to the moment when we encountered in mid-ocean something like a river with a violent current. My ship was last. The others sailed on and gradually, as each one entered this place, they disappeared and did not come back. We do not know what happened to them. As for me, I returned where I was and did not enter that current.

"But the emperor did not want to believe him. He equipped two thousand vessels, a thousand for himself and the men who accompanied him, and a thousand for water and supplies. He conferred power on me and left with his companions on the ocean. This was the last time that I saw him and the others, and I remained absolute ruler of the empire."

A fleet of 2000 watercraft may appear an exaggeration but the availability of such large fleets has often been reported in chronicles on West Africa. In 1591, Askia Ishaq, the last of the Songhay emperors, used close to 3000 boats to evacuate Gao, his capital, in the face of an invading Moroccan army.[30]

I have presented evidence in a dozen categories to establish that there were Africans in America before Columbus. If European or Asiatic* visitors were involved, one or two categories of evidence would have been considered enough. I have, over the last twenty-one years, presented a dozen European witnesses, including Columbus himself, in addition to metallurgical evidence, linguistic evidence, botanical evidence, cartographic evidence, skeletal evidence, epigraphic evidence (i.e. a script used in a region from which the humans attached to the skeletons came) oceanographic evidence (marine conveyor belts) navigational evidence (ancient boats tested in our time on those currents or belts) iconographic evidence (about half a hundred surviving sculptures and paintings with identifiable racial markers), African oral evidence supported by identical Arab documentary evidence. The evidence does not relate to disconnected events or widely disconnected phases of time. It would be difficult to find any historical event that goes back to 1310 that presents us with evidence in all of these diverse categories.

But it is not only the matter but the manner in which the case was presented that has been the subject of attack by my critics. They have confused method with substance and have referred to the dramatized openings of chapters in *They Came Before Columbus* as "scenarios." The word is meant to suggest that both the manner and matter is novelistic, that is, invented, fictionalized. This is a dishonest characterization.

---

*As readers will see in chapter 3, the Chinese are now being projected as the most probable purveyors of ancient American cocaine to the ancient Egyptians, even though *the Egyptians*, not the Chinese, *have a pre–Christian map of the Atlantic coast of South America and the Gulf of Mexico* and even though the cocaine has been detected in ancient Egyptian mummies, not Chinese mummies. Recent discoveries show all the variants of the African in ancient Egyptian graves.

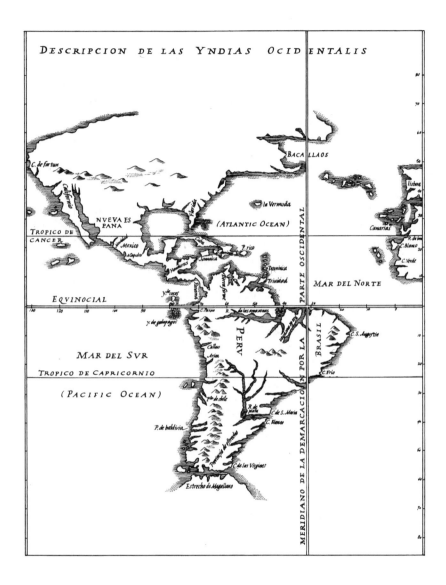

The Tordesillas line. Drawn at the request of King Don Juan of Portugal in June, 1494, before the European discovery of South America, on the strength of information gleaned from African mariners in Guinea. The line is 375 leagues west of the Cape Verde islands (about 1680 miles, using Vespucci's measurement of a league) and was later seen to include roughly 200 miles of Brazil.

It was through the meticulous examination of historical narratives that I was galvanized by a desire to draw the reader into the living skin of lost times and thus adopted a dramatic mode of presentation as curtain openers to most chapters. The facts were well researched, notes indicating the archival sources were always given, the skeletal data buried in musty volumes were fleshed and animated with startling but authentic moments of history. This is a method used by the best of historians to bring a vanished world and ghostly figures to life. Used sparingly and cautiously, and with a respect for the authenticity of detail, it can make a difference between opening a door to the past or closing it to all but a few.

This method brought life stirring afresh from the tombs of the archives. The curtain lifted on Columbus sitting at dinner in the court of King John II in the valley of Paraiso. Concentrated in that single selected incident, we can see the personal ambitions and duplicities of the man, the intrigues and rivalries of the powers that were about to alter the destiny of Africa and America.[31]

When I entered the world of medieval Mali in the early fourteenth century, it was with the telescopic lens of the historian and the microscopic focus of the novelist. I found it was the only way to see, in the broadest and yet most intimate terms, the life of the Mandingo king Abu Bakari II and the life of his court at Niani on the banks of the Sankarini river. Every detail of this court was drawn from first hand travellers' accounts. They were not created for the purpose of drama but dramatized for the purpose of recreation.[32]

In like manner one should look at the evocation of medieval Tlatelulco with the mist of morning over the lake, the hollow scream of the conches, the crack of the fisherman's paddle on the glass of the water, the ash and bloom of the volcanoes sleeping in the clouds.[33] I was thrilled to receive a letter from someone who had lived there, had awakened at morning like my Aztec featherworker on the edge of the lake, had watched the volcano fusing its distant wisp of smoke with a passing cloud (an eminent authority, moreover, on Mexican colonial art, Judy de Sandoval). My method was fully vindicated when she wrote saying that she was so moved by the authenticity of the description of her childhood village that she wept. I have never seen Sandoval's village and I want to emphasize this in order to show the care with which I have applied this method and technique to dead documents in my attempt to breathe life into ancient peoples and places, times through which we can no longer pass, streets on which we may not walk again, worlds we can no longer visit.

Notes

1. *Race, Discourse and Origin of the Americas* (eds. Rex Nettleford and Vera Hyatt) Smithsonian Institution Press, 1995
2. "Van Sertima's Afrocentricity and the Olmecs"—Bernard Ortiz de Montellano, Warren Barbour, and Gabriel Haslip Viera, *Current Anthropology, June 1997.*
3. Ibid.
4. "Van Sertima's Address to the Congressional Committee overseeing the work of the Christopher Columbus Quincentenary Commission"—*Congressional Records. July 7, 1987.*
5. *Raccolta. Parte 1. Vol. 1*, as quoted in *Christopher Columbus, His Life, His Work, His Remains* by John Boyd Thacher, 1903—4:2 380)
6. "Mandinga Voyages Across the Atlantic" by Harold Lawrence in *African Presence in Early America—Journal of African Civilizations*, Vol. 8, No. 2, 1986, p. 179.
7. *Modern Dictionary: Arabic English* by E.A. and E.E. Elias, Cairo, Elias Modern Press, 1962–63, p. 485–486.
8. *The Life of Christopher Columbus* by Ferdinand Columbus (Translated and annotated by Benjamin Keen) Rutgers University Press, New Brunswick, New Jersey, 1959, p, 234.
9. *Historia de Mexico.* by Lopez de Gomara, Anvers, 1554.
10. *De Orbo Novo: The Eight Decades of Peter Martyr d'Anghera*, F.A. MacNutt, Editor and Translator, New York, 1912
11. Popul Vuh: Le Livre Sacre et les Mythes de l'Antiquité Americaine, L'Abbé Brasseur de Bourbourg, Paris, 1861.
12. Ibid.
13. *Golden Age of the Moor, Journal of African Civilizations*, Vol. 2, edited by Ivan Van Sertima, 1991.
14. John Boyd Thacher, *Christopher Columbus, His Life. His Work, His Remains.* New York, G.P. Putnam's Sons, 1903, vol. 2, p. 380
15. De Quatrefages, *Histoire Generale des Races Humaines: Introduction à l'Étude des Races Humaines.* Paris, A. Hennuyer, 1889.
16. Peter de Roo, *History of America Before Columbus*, London and Philadelphia, J.P. Lippincott, 1900, p. 302.
17. C.S. Rafinesque, *The American Nations: or an Outline of a National History of the Ancient and Modern Nations of North and South America.*, vol. 1, pp. 121, 186–187, 194, 208–209 (Philadelphia 1832/33)
18. Charles L.G. Anderson, *Life and Letters of Vasco Nuñez de Balboa* (New York, Fleming H. Revel Co., 1941, p. 163)
19. Alexander Von Wuthenau, *The Art of Terracotta Pottery in pre-Columbian South and Central America*, New York: Crown, 1969.
20. S.G. Stephens, "Transoceanic Dispersal of New World Cottons" in Riley, Kelley, Pennington and Rands (eds) *Man across the Sea*, Austin, University of Texas Press, 1971,p. 413.
21. David Kelley in *Race, Discourse and Origin of the Americas*, Smithsonian Institution Press, 1995.

22. See Spanish painting of the Africans under Boabdil surrendering in Granada on January 2, 1492, in *Golden Age of the Moor* (ed. Van Sertima, JAC Vol. II, 1991)
23. John Boyd Thacher, *Christopher Columbus, His Life, His Work, His Remains*, New York, G.P. Putnam's Sons, 1903, Vol. 2, p. 379.
24. Harold Lawrence, "Mandingo Voyages Across the Atlantic" in *African Presence in Early America* (*Journal of African Civilizations*, vol. 8, no. 2).
25. John Boyd Thacher, ibid., 1903, Vol. 1, p. 665. Also see Van Sertima, *They Came Before Columbus*, Random House, 1976, p. 5–10.
26. See also Van Sertima's Op-Ed article in the *New York Times* of Dec.4, 1975—"Archeology's Discovery of an African Presence in America", subtitled by the *Times* "Bad News for Columbus". This article reports, among other things, the discovery of two male African skeletons in the U.S. Virgin Islands in a grave dated A.D. 1250. The Associated Press had reported in the *Washington Post* earlier that year that American scientists had discovered skeletons of two male Africans in an A.D. 1250 grave at St Thomas (U.S. Virgin Islands). Clamped around the forearm of one of these was a pre-Columbian ceramic ornament. The report also revealed that a peculiar dental ritual associated with some Africans along the Atlantic coast—"filing of incisor teeth" had been noted. Yet 22 years later, hoping that details of this report were long forgotten, a "scientist" in the U.S. Virgin Islands issued a report that these Africans were really found to have "dental disease". This was proof, according to Capt. Jim McManus that they came *after* Columbus since dental disease cannot occur among "primitives" who had not yet tasted "the sweet diet of civilization." (exact quotes) The pre-Columbian ornament, he declared, countering the report of those who first examined the grave must be (especially in the light of their post-Columbus dental disease) nothing more than "an accidental association". This "Johnny-come-lately" seems to be unaware of the interview and report by the Associated Press and my follow-up investigation in person twenty-one years ago. He is unaware also of the Old World script found above the rockpool at St John, which has been deciphered by two independent authorities (see photo)
27. "Africans across the Sea", chapter 4, *They Came Before Columbus*
28. Ivan Van Sertima "Tribute to a Departed Scholar" in *Egypt: Child of Africa*, Vol. 12, *Journal of African Civilizations*, 1995, p. 239, 240
29. *They Came Before Columbus*, p. xiv, xv.
30. Harold Lawrence, "Mandingo Voyages Across the Atlantic" in *Journal of African Civilizations*, vol. 8, no. 2, 1986, pp. 170, 174.
31. See ch. 1, *They Came Before Columbus*.
32. See ch. 3, *They Came Before Columbus*, pp. 37–49.
33. See note 30

This painting from the tomb of Ramses III (1200 B.C.) shows that the Egyptians saw themselves as Blacks, and painted themselves as such without possible confusion with the Indo-Europeans [Caucasoids] or the Semites. It is a representation of the races in their most minute differences, which insures the accuracy of the colors. Throughout their entire history, the Egyptians never entertained the fantasy of portraying themselves by types B or D.

A) The Egyptian seen by himself, black type   C) The other Blacks in Africa
B) The "Indo-European"   D) The Semite

(From K. R. Lepsius: Denkmaler aus Aegypten und Aethioien, Erganzungsband, plate 48)

2

Physical and Ritual Evidence of Egyptian-Nubian Contact in the Time of the Ramessides

Egyptian-Nubian Contact with the Olmec c. 1200 B.C.

*Van Sertima's expedition allegedly sailed or
drifted westward to the Gulf of Mexico where
it came in contact with inferior Olmecs. These
individuals created Olmec civilization.*
—*De Montellano, Barbour and Haslip-
Viera, Current Anthropology, 1997*

All significant contact between two peoples inevitably lead to influences. To accuse me of calling the Olmec people "inferior" simply because I have demonstrated that people from another land and culture made contact with them earlier than Europeans and that this contact led to certain influences, is to exhibit a facile, narrow, racist vision of the multiple heritage and crosscultural history of man. There is no question, for example, that Europe had a profound influence on Africa and America after 1492. Everyone accepts that. To show, however, that the medieval Moors—Africans and Arabs—had a profound influence on Spain, Portugal and Sicily, from the eighth to the fifteenth century (711-1492)[1] would be vehemently resisted since it would establish a fundamental balance and equality among the varied "races" of man and demonstrate once again the natural give and take of humans in the connected rooms of this global house, from today's familiar to yesteryear's forgotten centuries. It would also upset the smug assumption that Africans went nowhere outside the primeval jungle until Europe mercifully lifted them up and found new homes for them in this brand "new world", a world "discovered" by Columbus in the very same year the Moors surrendered in Granada.[2] (see photo on p. 8, chapter 1)

Let me say, first of all, I have never referred to the Olmec as "inferior". I have the profoundest respect for native Americans. I come from a country named by them—Guyana—"land of waters". I grew up among them. *I am one of them*, part Macusi Indian and part African. My critics claim that I have trampled upon the self-respect and self-esteem of native Americans and they have come forward to champion their cause. America's original people, my people, would be horrified to have as champions of our cause, De Montellano, Barbour, and Haslip-Viera, who disgrace us with the charge that "native Americans would have sacrificed and eaten Africans if they came."[3]

As far back as 1976 I made it very clear that I was not suggesting that Africans founded native American civilization. That is so absurd that even an idiot would not give it a second thought. Let me quote from *They Came Before Columbus* published eariler in that year.

"I think it necessary to make it clear—since partisan and ethnocentric scholarship is the order of the day—that the emergence of the Negroid face, which the archeological and cultural data overwhelmingly confirm, in no way presupposes the lack of a native originality, the absence of other influences or the automatic eclipse of other faces".[4] Ten years later, in 1986, I state this with even greater force: "I cannot subscribe to the notion that civilization suddenly dropped onto the American earth from the Egyptian heaven."[5]

Far more serious than this misrepresentation, however, is the ignorance displayed by my critics with regard to the physiognomic traits of African people in general and ancient Egyptians in particular. *"None of the early Egyptians and Nubians looked like Negroes,"* they declare. *"They have long, narrow noses. Short, flat noses are confined to the West African ancestors of African Americans".*[6] I know this sounds incredible, coming as it does from three "savants" posing as professors of history and anthropology, but I am quoting them "word for word" from a copy of the original document sent to me by *Current Anthro-*

---

*This statement appears in version that was sent to me. Reasons why I withdrew my "detailed response" are given in the Appendix to this book.

pology. I have edited and published four books on Egypt,[7] illustrated by about a hundred faces of the ancient Egyptian and Nubian. I hereby offer them a lecture on the variants of the African, replete with ancient and authentic images. I offer it to them out of a humanitarian concern since I would not wish even my worst enemy to appear so indecently clad in a transparent garment of racist follies.

Dr. Keith Crawford shows in an essay *"Racial Identity of Egyptian populations based on an Analysis of Physical Remains"*[8] that the placing of the African into a facile single-type classification to determine the race of the Nile Valley inhabitants has led to the grossest falsifications imaginable. No single myth in this whole field of study has done more damage than the monotypic classification of the African or Africoid.

Native African populations are phenotypically "polytypic", that is, there exists in Africa a variety of phenotypes (faces and/or body shapes) that may differ from the stereotypical "Negro", falsely formed and firmly fixed within the rigid imagination and classification of Eurocentric observers. There are at least six of these African variants or types. I shall, lest they be lost to my uninformed critics, highlight the main features of these variants or types. There is the *Elongated* variant, to which General Aidid, who fought American troops to a standoff in Somalia a few years ago, belongs. This variant is distinguished by an elongated body build, narrow head, face and nose, dark skin and spiralled hair, thick but not everted lips. They range from long to moderately long-headed with a narrow nasal opening, long narrow face and mild to absent prognathism (that is, with either slightly protruding or non-protruding upper jaw/lower face) This stands in contrast to the classical Negro type but are indigenous, unmixed Africans. They were living in Africa long before dynastic Egypt was born. The Elongated type includes the Fulani, the Tutsi and the Hima (Rwanda) the Masai (Kenya) the Galla (Ethiopia) the Somalis (Somalia) and the Beja (Northern Sudan) (see photo).

Then there is the *Nilotic* variant who is taller than the Elongated type with a narrower head, a lower and wider nose, a very slender body, with extremely long legs and little fat. These Nilotic types include the Nuer, the Dinka, the Shilluk and the Anuak, all of whom occupy the Nile River basins of the Southern Sudan.(see photo) Most popular, of course, is that variant which innocents and experts alike foolishly refer to as the "true Negro." This variant is said to have skin

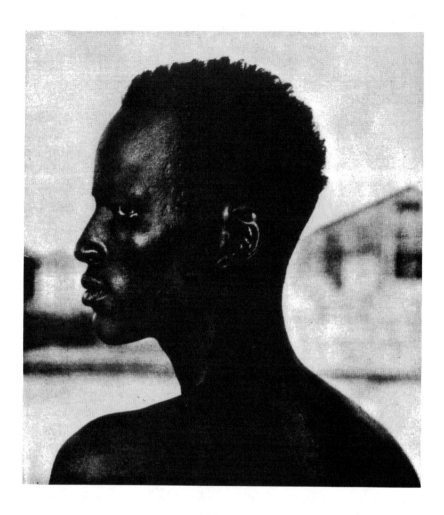

Figure 1. An Africoid of the "Elongated" variety. Africans with these facial features were labelled "Hamitic" and were thought to have Caucasoid admixture or even to belong to the Caucasoid race. Genetic analysis and ancestral relationships show many populations with these features to cluster with other African populations and emerge distinct from European or Asiatic races (From Coon, C., 1965).

Figure 2. An Africoid of the "Broad" variety (A Nuba chief from Kenya). Africans with these features were termed "Negroes" and populations with these characteristics were often assumed to represent the only "pure" unmixed members of the race. In actuality, this is only one of many "true" Africoid variants. Africoids display a tremendous degree of variability but are more closely related to each other than to any populations outside of Africa (From Van Sertima, 1979)

Figure 3. An Africoid of the "Nilotic" variety. Models on racial differentiation that are scientifically invalid attribute certain facial features to Caucasoid influence, yet these modern populations show no blood group characteristics or any other genetic features that would relate them to Caucasoid populations (From Coon, C., 1965).

color varying from dark brown to black, to be relatively long-armed and long-legged, of tall stature, broad shoulders, narrow hips, black and kinky hair, short, broad face, a considerable degree of prognathism (that is. with a jutting jaw or jutting lower face) flat nose, very depressed at the root, thick and often everted lips. (see photo) There are also the pygmies, whose skin is reddish-yellow to light-brown, broad-headed with very wide nose. One must also make mention of the so-called *"Bushman"* variant, which is hard to box and bind into a single phenotype. This variant shows a remarkable degree of heterogeneity or diversity. Their types range from dark to light complexions, long to moderately long heads, pronounced to absent lower face protrusion. We may cite one or two more types, like the Khartoum variant, but these should suffice. They were *all* found in ancient Egyptian graves or in mummy wrappings or in statuary.

On the matter of the race of the Egyptians and Nubians and their phenotypes, my critics have stumbled very badly. They refer to works they have read hastily and superficially. They give the impression that the work of scholars like Ucko, A.C. Berry, and R.J. Berry, established that the racial composition of both ancient and modern Egypt was roughly the same. They point out what has already been pointed out in the Journal I edit[9] that there is a remarkable degree of homogeneity in this area for 5000 years. Because they have flashed through these volumes in unscholarly haste in order to confirm their ill-founded hypothesis on the peoples of ancient Egypt, they fail to notice that the curtain falls on this 5000–year period with the close of the native dynasties, *before* the mixings ushered in by the Assyrian, Persian, Greek, Roman, and Arab invaders, not to mention the English and French colonial powers. What they also fail to mention is that the study also showed an amazing closeness to the iron age Jebel Maya Nubian population, which Strouhal, Arkell and others had described as "Negro". The word "African" or "Africoid" here is more preferable, since the monotypic classification of Africans has led to serious problems.

What my critics had hoped to gain by mentioning the 5000 years of homogeneity without noting when the 5000 year period ended, was a counter to "Afrocentrics who argue that modern populations of Egyptians and Nubians look different from those of antiquity". *They certainly do!* Who do they expect to believe that, after the influx of millions of foriegners and half a dozen invasions (Hyksos, Assyrians,

Persians, Greeks, Romans, Arabs) today's Egyptians would look like the blacks of modern Africa? It would be as absurd as comparing the Americans who came across the Bering Straits with the Americans of today. No DNA analysis by Cavalli-Sforza, Menotti, and Piazza which they dishonestly cite, in their facile counter-argument, can establish such a groundless proposition. Work done in this field by Thoma, Ferembach, Wendorf, Stewart, Greene and Armelagos, Rightmore, Keita and Crawford expose this as pure nonsense. Let us look at what these serious archeologists have said about the races of ancient Egypt for we are not discussing the modern period. We are dealing with the dynastic Egyptians and Nubians and their relationship to early Africa.

The earliest human fossil found in Egypt was the skeleton of the Nazlet Khater man found near Tahta, Egypt which was dated to 35,000–30,000 B.C. (upper Paleolithic period). Regarding the racial affinity of this skeleton, *Thoma* (1984) concludes.

"Strong alveolar prognathism combined with fossa praenasalis in an African skull is suggestive of Negroid morphology. The radio-humeral index of Nazlet Khater man is the same as the mean of Taforalt (76.6). According to *Ferembach* (1962) "this value is near to the Negroid average".

In 1982 Wendorf discovered a skeleton at Wadi Kubbaniya, located 10-15 kilometers north of Aswan in Egypt.This skeleton dated to approximately 20,000 B.C. The wide nasal aperture, lower nasal margin morphology (presence of the sulcus praenasalis) wide interorbital distance and alveolar prognathism demonstrate affinities with Broad African variants (i.e., Negroid traits) *Stewart* (1985) *Greene* and *Armelagos* (1964) analyzed a collection of crania from Wadi Halfa, dating from 13,000 to 8,000 b.C. The skulls were doliocephalic with bun-shaped occiputs, and they displayed extreme facial flattening in the orbital and nasal regions, massive browridges, sloping foreheads, great alveolar prognathism, large teeth and large, deep mandibles. *Rightmore* (1975) notes a similarity between this population and skeletons from West Africa (Tamaya Mellet, Niger and El Guettara, Mali)[10] (Keith Crawford, 1995).

These studies indicate the presence of populations with Broad African traits (Negroid) as the earliest inhabitants of Egypt. Modifications of this early type did occur but, in the 5000-year period upon which we are focussing, these modifications were due to an interplay between African variants (the Elongated variant, in particular, misclassified as "Hamitic"). Strangely enough, when few Europeans were aware of the wonders of ancient Egypt, the mythical sons of Ham (Hamites) were thought of as "Blacks" but the moment they began to enter Egypt in great numbers following the Napoleonic expedition of 1798, they raised their eyes in incredulous wonder at the marvels of this civilization and there arose "the historical impetus to transform the Hamites into Caucasians.[11] One of Cheikh Anta Diop's sarcastic remarks on these myth-makers, who sought to erase the Black from Egyptian history so that they could claim it, is worth quoting: "They have invented the ingenious, convenient, fictional notion of the 'true Negro' which allows them to consider all the real negroes on this earth as fake Negroes".

Here follows a series of ancient Egyptian and Nubian royalty and commoners, who, according to the racial experts (Bernard Ortiz de Montellano, Warren Barbour and Gabriel Haslip-Viera) had only "long, narrow noses" unlike the "short, flat-nosed ancestors of African-Americans". According to these three wise men, Egyptians and Nubians were never "tainted" by African blood, never were a composite of African variants or phenotypes, and could not possibly have been models for some of the "Negro-looking" stone heads. These heads were "spitting images of the native" (de Montellano) or represented "ball-players" (Encyclopedia Brittanica) or were were-jaguars, (Aguirre Beltran) or, if some of them appeared in pre-Columbian American terracotta, looking even more realistically like Negroes, then they were not genuine sculptures at all but probably "forged artifacts". (De Montellano et al.)

Narmer-Menes, first historic king of Egypt, creator of the dynastic system, the delta, and the city of Memphis; circa 3168 B.C. *Courtesy of Wayne Chandler and Gaynell Catherine.*

Close up of Osiris, showing negroid features. *Courtesy of Wayne Chandler and Gaynell Catherine.*

Old Kingdom statue of Isis and Horus, the original black madonna, dated circa 2635 B.C. *Courtesy of Wayne Chandler and Gaynell Catherine.*

Bas relief of King Djoser, circa 2635 B.C. *Courtesy of Wayne Chandler and Gaynell Catherine.*

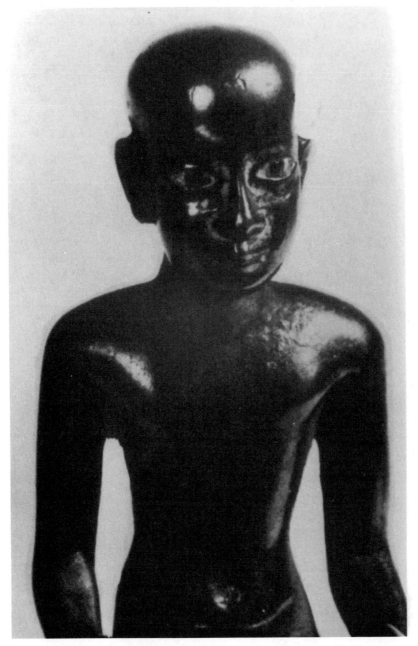

Close up of Old Kingdom statuette of Imhotep, showing pronounced negroid features. *Courtesy of Wayne Chandler and Gaynell Catherine.*

Bas-relief of daily life. *Courtesy of Wayne Chandler and Gaynell Catherine.*

Old Kingdom bas-relief of women making perfume. (Notice both facial features and braided hair) *Courtesy of Wayne Chandler and Gaynell Catherine.*

Khufu (Cheops), King of the Fourth Dynasty, builder of the Great Pyramid. *Courtesy of Wayne Chandler and Gaynell Catherine.*

Khafre or Chephren, builder of the Second Great Pyramid of Gizeh.
Courtesy of Wayne Chandler and Gaynell Catherine.

Thutmosis III

Nubian pharaoh Ushanaru on Sinjirli stele

Relief of Nubian pharaoh Taharka from Kawa Temples

Nubian pharaoh Shabaka

Nubian pharaoh Tanwetamani
(All Nubian photos are by courtesy of Peggy Bertram, author of the forthcoming book *Return to Kawa*)

Before we leave the question of the race of the ancient Egyptian and Nubian, it is important that we highlight the most definitive proof of the predominant race of Egypt in the first contact period 1200 B.C. The color photograph we present exposes the ignorance of our critics with regard to this most disputed issue. It is a painting from the tomb of Ramses III (1200 B.C.) It shows that the Egyptians (at A) saw themselves in that period as no different from the Nubian and other Blacks (at C) They painted themselves as such without confusion with the Indo-Europeans or Caucasoids (at B) or the Semites (at D). It is a realistic representation of the races in their most minute differences at that point in time. Study it closely. Note how the angle of protrusion of the nose and lips as well as the hair texture and the clothing, not just the shade of skin, distinguish the Blacks at A and C from the Indo-European and the Semite at B and D. Note also the minute distinctions made in power relations in 1200 B.C. The Egyptian at that time is the leading power in the world. Second in power is the Indo-European. Third is the Nubian who does not come to full ascendancy until the 25th dynasty and, though not distinguished from the Egyptian in racial terms, is shown to have less power and status than the Egyptian at that point in time. He is dressed in identical costume but sports "two" tassels or banners from his tunic instead of the Egyptian three. (see photo from K.R. Lepsius: *Denkmaler aus Aegypten und Aethiopien*, Erganzungsband, plate 48)

This extended discourse and photo-display on the predominant race of the ancient Egyptians and Nubians is of great relevance in a study of the stone heads found among the Olmec. Not all of these heads are African. I have said that over and over again. I have never claimed that Africans carved these heads or that they were the only models for them. What I have claimed, and this cannot be disputed, except by *the simple-minded or the Afrophobic*, (and statements by my critics show again and again that they fall well within the latter category) is (a) that the skull and skeletal evidence examined in certain Olmec settlements show a distinct African physical presence *among them* (b) that this alien presence is displayed not only in bones but in the features of *some* of the Olmec stones (c) that it is evident in a startling range of unique and complex rituals which appear nowhere else in the world, and in such a combination save in Egypto-Nubian civilization and (d) that these unique and complex rituals have such clear antecedence in the one, that they defy such a range of duplication, *without contact*, in the other.

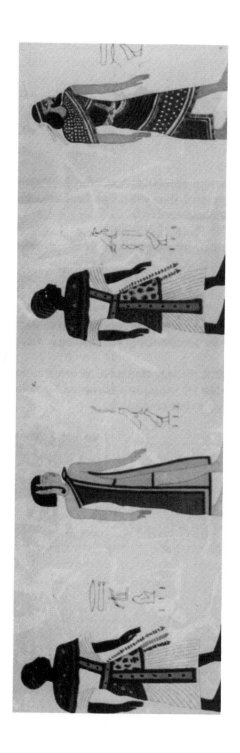

This painting from the tomb of Ramses III (1200 B.C.) shows that the Egyptians saw themselves as Blacks, and painted themselves as such without possible confusion with the Indo-Europeans [Caucasoids] or the Semites. It is a representation of the races in their most minute differences, which insures the accuracy of the colors. Throughout their entire history, the Egyptians never entertained the fantasy of portraying themselves by types B or D.

A) The Egyptian seen by himself, black type
B) The "Indo-European"
C) The other Blacks in Africa
D) The Semite

(From K. R. Lepsius: Denkmaler aus Aegypten und Aethioien, Erganzungsband, plate 48)
Note: The color version of this photo may be found on p. 30.

Now come the questions. What could have been the *motive* for such a journey to the other end of the world? And what *capacity* did the Egyptians have at that point in time to cross the Pacific or Atlantic oceans? Rafique Jairazbhoy has dealt more effectively than anyone with the first question—the question of motive. I shall return to that in a moment. I think he has overstated the influence of the Egyptian on the Olmec, going almost as far as to suggest that they "founded" Olmec civilization. My critics have attributed that claim to me. *Let me repeat: I have never ever said so.* But let me give this brilliant Indian scholar his due. He has, over the last quarter of a century, assiduously and painstakingly, pointed to an impressive body of unique and complex ritual parallels between the Olmec and the Egyptian. I think, however, he overstates the case, although he was nearer the mark than I was with respect to the dating of *the very first contact.* Carbon datings have changed and, in the light of this, the major Nubian contact is later. *However, it does not invalidate the claims I have made with regard to Egypto-Nubian influences, since the ritual complex I have outlined is duplicated in almost every aspect in both periods and among these intimately related peoples.* A meticulous examination of these parallels circa 1200 B.C. turns up only one possible exception— human-headed coffins. These have been found both in Argin, Nubia and in Olmec Mexico. No example of this Nubian feature has turned up *so far* in Egypt circa 1200 B.C. But it is important to point out also that Nubians would have been members of any major Egyptian expedition of that nature and at that earlier point in time (c. 1200 B.C.)

Let it also be noted, that carbon datings have changed as dramatically in the Old World as they have in the New. Nubia has emerged, in the light of new archeological discoveries, not simply as a latecomer to pharaonic civilization but as its actual birthplace. These new datings and discoveries in the Egypto-Nubian world, most of which were revealed after the publication of *They Came Before Columbus*, (1977) have reinforced my claims as to the importance of Nubia in any study of this matter of cultural transfers from the Old World to the New, regardless of whether it was c. 1200 B.C. or the later contact period. It is now known that pharaonic civilization did not begin in Egypt but in Nubia as early as 3,500 B.C. The first appearance of pharaohs, at Ta-Seti in Nubia, was revealed to the world eighteen years ago.[12] See also Bruce Williams "The Lost Pharaohs of Nubia" which was reprinted in *Egypt Revisited*.[13] Also, Timothy Kendall (*Meroitica*, 1996) cites 16 Nubian pharaohs who preceded those of the 25th dynasty (that is, well before the eighth century B.C.)[14] G.A. Reisner found Napatan pharaonic tombs in uninterrupted sequence at El Kurru well before 1000 B.C.

But to return to the question of motive and capacity for a transoceanic journey. We can establish with a considerable amount of evidence that the capacity for transoceanic journeys existed in ancient times and we shall give a brief overview of some of the ships that were available to the Egyptians as well as even harder evidence(an ancient map of South America when it was not artificially divided from North America by the Panama Canal) but we can only conjecture about the motive. In the case of the Egyptian sea journey to the land of Punt in East Africa, for example, it is clear that the motive for far journeys to strange lands was trade and possible expansion of empire. In the case of the journey across an ocean (primarily the Atlantic, as the Piri Re'is map [see photo in chapter 3] clearly shows) presenting us with formidably accurate and pre-modern data on the adjacent American and Atlantic coasts, we are in all likelihood dealing with a motive that transcends just the considerations of trade and imperial ambition.

Rafique Jairazbhoy, in his study of ancient Egyptians in America, presents us with the most plausible motive and backs up his conclusion with a very detailed examination of archeological evidence in America and Egypt circa 1200 B.C. The motive, as he has so ably demonstrated, went beyond trade or imperial ambitions. It was primarily religious. We are apt in our times to dismiss such motives but we are not talking about our times. Religion—the belief, for example, that the Pharaoh was God's representative upon the earth, that the bird in his upper crown represented his mastery of the Upper World and the serpent in the lower crown, sovereignty over the Lower Realm—is to be taken very seriously. Man's belief—whether of something imaginary or real—can turn him into the greatest force for good or evil. In the case of the Egyptians, it made them do things that we have never done again. The modern Japanese, for example, with all their vaunted technological mastery, found they could not build a pyramid rivalling even the minor ones the ancient Egyptians built. Wayne Chandler's detailed study of all the data documenting the Japanese attempt is eloquent proof of this.

"Upon beginning construction the Japanese found that they were faced with insurmountable problems. First and foremost, the duplicated hand tools the men were provided with could not cut the stone, so the workers had to resort to air jackhammers. Secondly, when the boulders were placed on the rafts another problem arose. They could not prevent the barges from capsizing, since they were soon overrun with water and could not be handled properly. They became unsafe for the men, due to the instability created by the weight of the rock. Therefore, the quarried boulders had to be transported across the Nile by steamboat. Upon reaching the shore they ran into a third problem: the limestone boulders began to sink into the river silt and sand of the desert, and those that did not sink were of no consequence for the men could not budge them.

"Once again modern technology was called upon in the way of trucks and land rovers to move the stone to the designated site. But the great numbers of men they had amassed could not lift the blocks by pulley, levers, nor ropes, and as a result, power cranes plus helicopters were contracted to do the job. Even then, employing the use of today's most powerful lifting machines, those blocks set in place were greatly out of alignment, and many (if not most) were broken, chipped, and badly scratched, due to improper handling.

"Finally, the Egyptian Government interceded and put an end to their agony. The unauthorized use of the heavy land equipment had torn asunder large stretches of desert land which had become quite an eye sore. The project was terminated and the pyramid (what little was intact) was dismantled. What the world learned from this endeavor were two things—one, that the "simple" methods conservative scholars have so long said were utilized were totally inadequate, falling way short of the mark—and two, even with the aid of modern technology in regards to transportation, lifting, quarrying, and placing these two-ton blocks the job done left much to be desired.

"In comparison, the ingenious masonry work exhibited in the construction of the pyramids, especially the Great Pyramid, far surpassed the meager attempts made by the Japanese. When archeologists removed one of the few remaining casing stones (the stones that at one time covered the entire pyramid) on the north side of the pyramid at its base they were shocked at what they discovered. None of the underlying blocks examined had chipped edges, cracks, or even scratches; they were perfect! In reference to the casing stones, one of the world's greatest Egyptologists, Flinders Petrie, found that the faces and butting surfaces of these 16-ton blocks were cut to 1/1000 of an inch of mathematical perfection.

He reported that "the mean variation of the cutting of the stone from a straight line and from a true square is but .01 inch in a length of 75 inches up the face, an amount of accuracy equal to most modern opticians' straight edges of such a length. These joints, with an area of some 35 square feet each, were not only worked as finely as this, but were cemented throughout. Though the stones were brought as close as as 1/500 of an inch, or, in fact, into contact, and the mean opening of the joint was 1/50 of an inch, yet the builders managed to fill the joint with cement, despite the great area of it, and the weight of the stone to be moved—some 16 tons. To merely place such stones in exact contact at the sides would be careful work, but to do so with cement in the joints seems almost impossible (Flinders Petrie, as quoted by Charles Smyth, *Our Inheritance in the Great Pyramid*, London, 1874, p.20) Thus the builders of these great monoliths quarried and cut stone within 1/1000 of an inch of mathematical perfection, and raised a man made mountain as meticulously as we cut gems.

There are approximately 2,300,000 blocks of stone which comprise the Great Pyramid. These individual blocks weigh from 2.5 tons to 70 tons (as much as a railroad locomotive) and originally covered an area of 13.1 acres. The Great Pyramid contains more stone than all the churches, chapels and cathedrals built in England since the time of Christ. If all the stone in this pyramid were sawed into blocks one foot on an edge and these were laid end to end, they would stretch two thirds of the way around the globe at the equator. The Great Pyramid contains enough stone to construct thirty Empire State Buildings".[15]

The most plausible motive for the great journey to "the far west of the world where the sun goes down" [America] lies in the religious belief of the ancient Egyptian priests and thinkers that therein "lay the entrance to the Underworld". Sahagun, in his study of ancient American oral tradition and the few manuscripts that survived the burning of early American books under the orders of Bishop de Landa, reports that settlers came to Mexico from across the sea and they came looking for a terrestial paradise—"Esta gente venia en demanda del paraiso terrenal."[16]

But what ships did the Egyptians have to make such journeys? And what ocean did they cross (the Pacific or the Atlantic?) in their quest for this imagined "entrance to the Underworld?" All the evidence— the ancient Piri Reis map found in the sacked library of Alexandria and the newly discovered relationship between ancient Egypt and the rest of Africa (especially West Africa) in pre-Christian times—points to the Atlantic. We shall deal with the Piri Reis map in very great detail when we come to chapter 3 (the section on South America) and we shall show, as Charles Hapgood and others have shown, that it was utterly impossible for anyone in the so called "age of Columbus" to have drawn such a map. Our first concern, however, since our critics see Egypt as an entity totally divorced, racially and culturally, from "darkest Africa" is to demonstrate the indisputable intimacy of the African-Egyptian connection in early times. It not only lies in the fact that all of the variants of the African are found in ancient Egyptian graves as we have shown but we have equally clear evidence of an ancient Egyptian connection with that part of Africa that borders the Atlantic coast. I shall here present just a selection of these ancient links.

The first was presented to UNESCO by Africa's leading scholar, Cheikh Anta Diop of Senegal. The charts to follow are a selection, demonstrating identicals and near-identicals between ancient Egyptian and Walaf, (spoken in Senegal, West Africa). The evidence of this connection was so overwhelming that Unesco scholars,who had opposed the suggestion that there was a profound and intimate connection between ancient Egyptian and African language and culture, were forced to retreat from their earlier positions. I quote from the UNESCO report.

On the subject of Egyptian culture: "Professor Vercoutter remarked that, in his view, Egypt was African in its way of writing, in its culture and in its way of thinking." Professor Leclant, for his part, "recognized the same African character in the Egyptian temperament and way of thinking".

In regard to linguistics (see charts on pages 62–65) it is stated in the UNESCO report that "this item, in contrast to those previously discussed, revealed a large measure of agreement among the participants. The report by Professors Diop and Obenga were regarded as being very constructive". Thus, some of the world's leading scholars who had, at first, on the strength of their early training and biases, opposed the conclusions of Diop and Obenga, were forced into a surrender of their earlier theories by what the UNESCO report calls "the painstakingly researched contributions of Professors Cheikh Anta Diop and Obenga."

The UNESCO symposium rejected the long-held theory that Pharaonic Egyptian was a Semitic language. "Turning to wider issues, Professor Sauneron drew attention to the interest of the method suggested by Professor Obenga following Professor Diop. Egyptian remained a stable language for a period of at least 4,500 years. Egypt was situated at a point of convergence of outside influences and it was to be expected that borrowing had been made from foriegn languages, but the Semitic roots numbered only a few hundred as compared with a total of several thousand words. The Egyptian language could not be isolated from its African context and its origin could not be explained in terms of Semitic."

The genetic, that is, the non-accidental relationship between Egyptian and the African languages was recognized: "Professor Sauneron noted that the method which had been used was of considerable interest, since it could not be purely fortuitous that there was a similarity between the third person singular suffixed pronouns in ancient Egyptian and in Wolof. He hoped that an attempt would be made to reconstitute a palaeo-African language, using present day languages as a starting point."

In the general conclusion to the UNESCO report it was stated that: "Although the preparatory working paper sent out by Unesco gave particulars of what was desired, none of the participants prepared communications comparable with the painstakingly researched contributions of Professors Cheikh Anta Diop and Obenga.[17]

The linguistic charts to follow show the intimate and ancient interconnection between the Egyptian and "inner Africa", in particular the links with Africans who were in proximity to the Atlantic ocean. This is a critical interconnection. For, not only is the Atlantic coast of Africa and the Atlantic coast of Mexico and the Atlantic coast of South America represented in an ancient Egyptian map found in the sacked library of Alexandria (the Piri Re'is map—see Section 3 on South America) but no one could possibly have made this map even two centuries after the so-called "discovery of America" by Columbus (*see why* in our detailed discussion of this map in Section 3). Not only that. It fits in perfectly with early Egyptian religious fantasies of "The Far West of the world where the sun goes down: Entrance to the Underworld".

Before we come to the charts of linguistic affinities (p. 62–65) that establish definitively a family relationship between languages of some of the Atlantic coast Africans and the Egyptians in ancient times, it is necessary to point to intercourse between these peoples long after their dispersal from a common womb and seed. G.A. Wainwright in the journal *Man* (October 1951, p. 133–135)[18] describes a ram-headed breast-plate from ancient Egypt found in an ancient context in Lagos, Nigeria. Lady Lugard, in chapter 26 of *A Tropical Dependency*[19] details for us the influence of ancient Egyptian Pharaohs in Hausaland. Even important to this discussion, is an ancient scientific èlite in West Africa—the Dogon of Mali—who probably escaped slavery by dint of their virtual invisibility in the high mountains. They were found to have had some connection with ancient Egypt. Their name for God (*Amma* for the Egyptian *Amon*) is just one of many examples of an early Egyptian connection. Their early astonishing discoveries in astronomy, which otherwise sane commentators (like Carl Sagan) attributed to the visit of "extraterrestrial" visitors to Africa may well have been due to their acquisition of the perfectly ground spherical crystal lenses found in ancient Egypt by the Russian scientist Volosimo. This discovery convinced the Russians that Galileo was not fantasizing when he said that the ancient Egyptians had telescopes. The Dogon trade link with the Egyptians may have led to an importation of these lenses, as some scholars have suggested, but Dogon discoveries go well beyond that of the Egyptians in relation to Sirius B—the invisible companion of the brightest star in the night sky, Sirius A. A brief summary of one of their discoveries is worth noting here:

"The Dogon knew that this star (Sirius B) although invisible to the naked eye, had an elliptical orbit around Sirius A that took 50 years to complete. Modern science confirms this orbit. The Dogon drew a diagram (see illustration) showing the course and trajectory of this star up unto the year 1990 (they were studied by Marcel Griaule from 1931–1956). Modern astronomical projections are identical with this. The Dogon say that this tiny star is composed of a metal heavier than iron and that if all the men on earth were a single lifting mechanism they could not budge it. Modern science confirms that.[20]

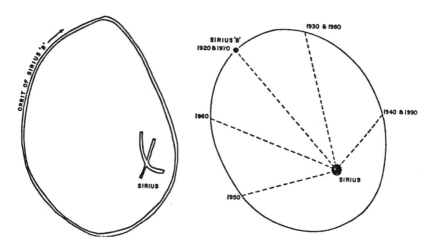

On the left a Dogon sand drawing of the orbit of Sirius B (Po Tolo) around Sirius; on the right, a modern astronomical drawing

From *Blacks in Science: Ancient and Modern*, Journal of African Civilizations, Vol. 5, 1983. Adams-Fig. 3

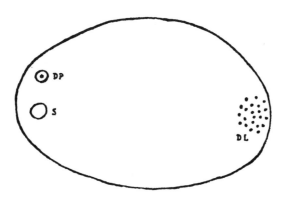

A drawing showing the trajectory of the star 'Po Tolo' (Sirius B) around Sirius. The small circle on the left marked S is Sirius. Above it the circle with the dot in the center is 'Po Tolo' (DP) in its closest position. At the other end of the oval the small cluster of dots (DL) represents the star at its most distant position from Sirius.

"African Observers of the Universe" in *Blacks in Science: Ancient and Modern*. Adams-Fig. 4

Now to return to the linguistic affinities that establish a family relationship between languages of some of the Atlantic coast Africans and the ancient Egyptians.

Below is a selection of linguistic affinities between Walaf, a Senegalese language spoken on the Atlantic coast of Africa, and ancient Egyptian to establish the interconnection between these worlds even before the 1200 B.C. Egyptian journey to the far west of the world (America).

Linguistic Affinity

Walaf, a Senegalese language spoken in the extreme west of Africa on the Atlantic Ocean, is perhaps as close to ancient Egyptian as Coptic. An exhaustive study of this question has recently been carried out. In this chapter enough is presented to show that the kinship between ancient Egyptian and the languages of Africa is not hypothetical but a demonstrable fact which it is impossible for modern scholarship to thrust aside.

As we shall see, the kinship is genealogical in nature.

EGYPTIAN	COPTIC	WALAF
𓆑 =kef=to grasp, to take a strip (of something)[64]	(Saïdique dialect) keh=to tame[65]	kef=seize a prey
PRESENT	**PRESENT**	**PRESENT**
kef i	keh	kef na
kef ek	keh ek	kef nga
kef et	keh ere	kef na
kef ef	kef ef	
kef es	keh es	kef ef na
		kef es
kef n	keh en	kef nanu
kef ton	keh etetû	kef ngen
kef sen[66]	keh ey	kef nañu
PAST	**PAST**	**PAST**
kef ni	keh nei	kef (on) na
kef (o) nek	keh nek	kef (on) nga
kef (o) net	keh nere	kef (on) na
kef (o) nef	keh nef	kef (on) ef na
kef (o) nes	keh nes	kef (on) es
kef (o) nen	keh nen	kef (on) nanu
kef (o) n ten	keh netsten	kef (on) ngen
kef (o) n sen[67]	keh ney[68]	kef (on) nañu

EGYPTIAN	WALAF
𓂻 =feh=go away	feh=rush off

We have the following correspondences between the verb forms, with identity or similarity of meaning: all the Egyptian verb forms, except for two, are also recorded in Walaf.

EGYPTIAN	WALAF
feh-ef	feh-ef
feh-es	feh-es
feh-n-ef	feh-ôn-ef
feh-n-es	feh-ônes
feh-w	feh-w
feh-wef	feh-w-ef
feh-w-es	feh-w-es
feh-w-n-ef	feh-w-ôn-ef
feh-w-n-es	feh-w-ôn-es
feh-in-ef	feh-il-ef
feh-in-es	feh-il-es
feh-t-ef	feh-t-ef
feh-t-es	feh-t-es
feh-tyfy	feh-ati-fy
feh-tysy	feh-at-ef
feh-tw-ef	mar-tw-ef
feh-tw-es	mar-tw-es
feh-kw(i)	fahi-kw
feh-n-tw-ef	feh-an-tw-ef
feh-n-tw-es	feh-an-tw-es
feh-y-ef	feh-y-ef
feh-y-es	fey-y-es
𓅘𓏜 = mer = love	mar = lick[69]
mer-ef	mar-ef
mer-es	mar-es
mer-n-ef	mar-ôn-ef
mer-n-es	mar-ôn-es
mer-w	mar-w
mer-w-ef	mar-w-ef
mer-w-n-f	mar-w-ôn-ef
mer-w-n-es	mar-w-ôn-es
mer-in-ef	mar-il-ef
mer-in-es	mar-il-es
mer-t-ef	mar-t-ef
mer-t-es	mar-t-es
mer-tw-ef	mar-tw-ef
mer-tw-es	mar-tw-es
mer-tyfy	mar-at-ef
mer-t-tysy	mar-at-es
	mar-aty-sy
	mar-aty-sy
mer-kwi	mari-kw

EGYPTIAN	WALAF
mer-y-ef	mar-y-ef
mer-y-es	mar-y-es
mer-n-tw-ef	mar-an-tw-ef
mer-n-tw-es	mar-antw-es
	mar-tw-ôn-ef
	mar-tw-ôn-es

Egyptian and Walaf Demonstratives

There are the following phonetic correspondences between Egyptian and Walaf demonstratives.

EGYPTIAN		WALAF
		ep→w
ᵒ᠍ = pw		p→b
	(ipw)→bw	w→w
ᵒ᠍ = pwy		p→b̄
	(ipw)→bwy	w→2
		y→y
ᵒ = pn	bané	p→b̄
	(ipn)→	n→n
	balé	p→b̄
		n→1[70]
ᵒ = pf	bafe	p→b
	(ipf)→	f→f
ᵒ᠍ = pf3→bafa		p→b̄
		f→f
		3→a
ᵒ᠍ = pfy		p→b̄
	(ipfy)→bafy	f→f
		y→y
ᵒ᠍ = p3→bâ		p→b
		3→á
ᵒ᠍ = iptw→baɾw		p→b
		ɾ→t
		w→w
ᵒ = iptn→batné		p→b
		ɾ→t
	Batalé	n→n
		n→1
ᵒ = iptf		
ᵒ = iptf→batafé		p→b̄
		ɾ→t
		f→f

(a) The correspondence n (E)→1 (W)

EGYPTIAN	WALAF
n	l
𓆑𓏏𓂧 = nad = ask	lad = ask
𓂝𓏤 = nah = protect	lah = protect
𓃀—𓃀𓊾 = ben ben = wellup	belbel = well up
𓏏𓈖𓏤 = teni = grow old	talé = important
𓏏𓆑𓈖𓏏 = tefnwt = the goddess born of Ra's spittle	tefnit = 'spit out'· a human being. teflit = spittle tefli = spitter
𓃀𓆙 = nebt = plait	let = plait nâb = to plait hair temporarily

(b) The correspondence h (E)→g (W)

EGYPTIAN	WALAF
h	g
𓎛𓈖 = hen = phallus	gen = phallus
𓎛𓏤𓈖 = hwn = adolescent	gwné } = adolescent goné
𓎛𓂋 = hor = Horus	gor = vir (? male ?)
𓎛𓂋 𓏤 = hor gwn = the youth Horus	gor gwne = young man (m.ã.m)

It is still early to talk with precision of the vocalic accompaniment of the Egyptian phonemes. But the way is open for the rediscovery of the vocalics of ancient Egyptian from comparative studies with the languages of Africa.

These phonetic correspondences above are not ascribable either to elementary affinity or to the general laws of the human mind for they are regular correspondences on outstanding points extending through an entire system, that of the demonstratives in the two languages and that of the verbal languages. It is through the application of such laws that it was possible to demonstrate the existence of the Indo-European linguistic family.

The comparison could be carried to show that the majority of the phonemes remain unchanged between the two languages.

Now we come to the question of the capacity of the Egyptian to cross the ocean. I have already dealt with oceangoing vessels used by pre-Columbian Africans in section 1, including the successful rebuilding of an ancient Egyptian-type vessel, the Ra 1, by the Buduma people of Lake Chad. This replica of an ancient papyrus reed boat crossed the Atlantic successfully in 1969. It was rebuilt for a second crossing by native Americans (the Aymara) correcting an earlier mistake, profiting from the first trial and error. Like the Buduma Africans, they made it across the Atlantic in this pre-Christian boat. What Heyerdahl had proven was that the most ancient of Egyptian ships, predecessors of even more sophisticated models, could have crossed the Atlantic. Moveover, the ancient Egyptians had mapped the Atlantic coasts of both America and Africa (the Gulf Coast of Mexico and the upper part of South America as well as the Atlantic coast of West Africa). They did this before Christ. We shall present the ancient Egyptian map as definitive proof of this and discuss it in great detail in chapter 3 when we come to deal with evidence for an Egyptian presence in South America. (We shall also show, by way of an addendum by Dr. Charles Finch, the malicious and deliberate distortion of the facts re the Piri Reis map by de Montellano et al).

But to return to ancient Egyptian boats. Even in the early predynastic times the Egyptians were building plank boats as well as papyrus boats. These plank boats were sewn together and their joints caulked with fiber. It was an extension of the method first used for the papyrus boats. By the dynastic period they could boast of boats as long as three car trains. It is recorded that the black African pharaoh Sneferu, at the close of the Third dynasty, made in a single year sixty ships that were 100 feet long and the following year built three with a bow to stern measurement of 170 feet.[22]

Even the ships of the Far East came heavily under the influence of ancient Egyptian navigation. Among these influences we may mention "the papyrus and reed boat, the steering oar, the quarter rudders, both the sheer and tripod mast, the square sail twice as high as wide, the boom at the foot of the sail, spoon-shaped hulls, transverse beams projecting through the hull sides and the central mat-covered cabin.[23]

Runoko Rashidi, in a research note "Royal Ships of the Pharoahs" published in Egypt: Child of Africa (*Journal of African Civilizations*, vol. 12) highlights ruins of ancient Egyptian ships which are critical to this discussion. "Around 2600 B.C., King Sneferu of Dynasty IV sent a fleet of forty ships to the Phoenician city of Byblos on the eastern Mediterranean seaboard to obtain cedar and other valuable woods. Forty vessels returned with enough logs to construct three 170 foot-long ships and a number of barges. In Dynasty V, King Sahure (c. 2485 B.C.) launched the first known sea expedition to the sacred African land of Punt, believed to be located along the coast of Somalia. The fleet returned from Punt with 80,000 measures of myrrh, 6000 units of electrum, 2,600 units of wood and 23,020 measures of unguent.

Several large boat pits have been identified from Dynasty IV at Giza and Abu Rawash during the successive reigns of Khufu (Cheops) and Khafre (Chephren). In the 1950's, two enormous pits were discovered along the southern side of the great pyramid of Khufu (c. 2575 B.C.) at Giza. The first of Khufu's ships was restored during a process that encompassed ten years. The restored ship, which consisted of 1,224 pieces of wood which had been partly dismantled and stacked in thirteen successive layers in the pit, measured 142 feet in length, more than sixteen feet in width, with a capacity of about forty tons. This has been identified as the world's oldest intact ship, and has been described as "a masterpiece of woodcraft that could sail today if put into water."

"In 1894 French engineer, geologist, and archeologist, Jacques Jean Marie de Morgan (1857-1924), Director of the Service of Antiquities, while excavating the pyramid complex of King Senusret 111 (c. 1860 B.C.) at Dashur, uncovered three well-preserved cedar ships, each about 32 feet long. During the fall of 1991 a team of archeologists from the University Museum, University of Pennsylvania, excavating in the desert near the ancient city of Aabdju (modern Abydos) 280 miles south of Cairo,made a sensational new discovery—an entire royal fleet of twelve wooden ships, each fifty to sixty feet long, buried in the sand eight miles from the Nile River, near the site of Shunet Ez-Zebib."[24]

This is just a brief selection from Rashidi's research note on "Royal Ships of the Pharaohs". To this I should add, as an addenda to my own chapter on "Africans Across the Sea" (chapter 4 of *They Came Before Columbus*), that in my London address on ancient navigation (1985) I presented evidence that Queen Hatshepsut's barge at Deir El Bahri dwarfed Lord Nelson's flagship at Trafalgar. The Santa Maria on which Columbus sailed to America did not represent any quantum leap in man's navigation of the world's waterroads.

Having established both motive and capacity and (as an Egyptian map presented in section 4 of this monograph will clearly show) both the embarkation point as well as the landing zone of the Old World voyagers, I shall now proceed to present pictorial evidence of their physical presence in America B.C. First, in sculptures of stone and clay, then in skulls and skeletons, all clearly distinguishable from the native Americans of that period. But let me say once again, since this is the main charge of my dishonest critics, a physical presence (as I here present in this section) and a ritual influence (as I shall present in the following section of this chapter) in no way suggests the founding or creation of American civilization. Only a zealot or a bigot would suggest that.

I have never claimed that *all* the stone heads were African. I pointed to some of them which meet all the criteria that a scientific classification of racial types would establish, without the slightest doubt, as such. Dr. Matthew Stirling, head of the first expedition sent out by the Smithsonian, came to the same initial conclusion. "Amazingly Negroid,"[25] were his words. Even the first discoverer of a colossal stone head in 1862, Jose Melgar, a native Mexican, was so struck by the African features that he wrote the first essay on the African presence in early America. Beatrice de la Fuente practically broke into lyrical prose when she saw the head I shall discuss shortly—the one with braids. She declared, in a moment of rare innocence, brought on by the kind of visual shock that sometimes shatters prejudices, "it is the most remote in physiognomy from our indigenous ancestors". In the very next moment she turned on her words in fear, startled by the voice of her own otherness. Frederick Peterson did the same when the furor my book caused led to pressures from his colleagues to retract his statement about "a strong Negroid substratum connected with the Olmec magicians."[26] These two-mouthed commentators should not be attacked. Academic survival is the motive behind their retractions.

Dr. Clarence Weiant was the first American archeologist in the field (1938). The head of the Smithsonian expedition, Dr. Matthew Stirling, was delayed for some reason. Dr. Weiant defended me in the New York Times against my British would-be executioner, Glyn Daniel. Daniel, by the way, had never even studied the Olmecs, and the *New York Times*, I was told by an informer, had to return his initial attack on my work since the first draft of his critique presented no credible counter-evidence. Dr Weiant's doctoral thesis revealed dozens of Africoid types at Tres Zapotes, terracotta more startlingly realistic in its portrayal of these types than all but one of the stone heads—the head with braids. Before I discuss that particular head, however, I would like to quote Dr Weiant's comments:

"Van Sertima's work," Dr. Weiant wrote[27] "is a summary of six or seven years of meticulous reasearch based upon archaeology, Egyptology, African history, oceanography, geology, astronomy, botany, rare Arabic and Chinese manuscripts, the letters and journals of early American explorers and the observations of physical anthropologists. As one who has been immersed in Mexican archeology for some 40 years and who participated in the excavation of the first of the giant heads, I must confess I am thoroughly convinced of the soundness of Van Sertima's conclusions."

I come now to the most unusual head found in the Olmec world—the stone head with African features and seven braids. My critics have had a field day with this one. "There is no evidence" they say "that ancient Africans ever braided their hair. This style comes from colonial and modern Ethiopia". I know many of my readers are blinking in disbelief at this point . Here are three trained anthropologists, supposedly "teaching" in American universities, joining together to write a major monograph related to the subject of Africans and Africa, claiming that Africans never braided their hair in ancient times (see photo to follow) and that all Nubians and Egyptians have "long narrow noses" and that "short, flat noses are confined to the West African ancestors of African Americans" (see photos preceding). The brazenness behind these absurdities lies in the confident but facile assumption that no ancient heads showing braids can be found in Egypt or Nubia and that no ancient Egyptian or Nubian statuary with broad noses survive. This confidence is based on three factors (a) none of these professors know anything about ancient Africa and Africans. Unlike me, they were trained in one theatre of the world and in one limited field (b) most of the noses of Egyptian statuary were smashed (c) museums were very selective in their display of African phenotypes in Egypt, making sure they did not acquire or purchase Negro-looking types of royal stature for public display. But they are not going to get away with this. I have edited four books on ancient Egypt in the last twelve years.[28] These works are not confined to the writings of Afrocentrics either. They include essays by 26 living European and Euro-American scholars. They even include one of the discoverers of Ta-Seti, the first pharaonic dynasty, which preceded the Egyptian. My critics, there-

Nubian Braids in Ancient Egyptian Wigs
These are from a small selection of wigs with Africoid hair used by royal
and religious personages in ancient Egypt. These were photographed by
Jacqueline Van Sertima in the *Cairo Musuem* (*Nubian Exhibition*) in
August, 1988.

Kushite on Shakaba ivories.

fore, are not going to get away with their warmed-over racist rubbish, posing as "current anthropology". They've chosen to fight me on the worst of all possible battlefields.

Let us first deal with braided hair which, according to my critics, never occured among Egyptians or Nubians until modern times.

Several more examples of braided hair in ancient Egypt and Nubia appear in Frank Snowden's *Before Color Prejudice* but I do not have permission to use them. This book, however, is still in print and should be read closely to show how ignorant our critics are of the racial situation in ancient times. They talk about "dated sources," not realizing that one does not cite a source because one thinks it is gospel but because more often than not, the particular fact one is quoting from the dated source has been crosschecked against current knowledge. Had they crosschecked their sources they would not be making such fanciful claims about the stone heads to avoid being exposed as frauds. I must note some of their claims related to pre-Columbian sculptures before I place the braided stone head on display.

1. De Montellano et al. gleefully cite an outlandish suggestion by,

or cited by, Beatrice de la Fuente, that the stone heads are not sculptures of persons at all but symbols of mythic beings[29] (de la Fuente,
1992, pp. 130-133)

2. They also cite the Readers Digest (1986, p 140) which suggest
that the terracotta (clay pieces) representing Negroid types are "forged
artifacts".[30] They are not aware, of course, that the Germans subjected
one of the Mandingo heads which Von Wuthenau claims to be pre-
Columbian, to therminoluminescence dating before purchasing it for
the Stavenhagen Museum and that Von Wuthenau himself subjected
several of his pieces to the same rigid tests.

With respect to the stone heads, they want to have it five ways to
make sure that the ugly suggestion of a Negroid element completely
disappears.

Apart from the suggestion (1) that it may not represent a human,
but a "mythic being" (de la Fuente's reputed escape route) they also
claim (2) that some of the heads were made of dark stone and it had
nothing to do with black people but the Olmecs associated volcanoes
with rain and fertility and so dark volcanic rocks would have had
symbolic import and would have been appropriate for important sculptures. (3) in the very next breath they point out that some of the
sculptures were actually made of white stone and they turned dark
over time. Still fearing that their readers might take these sculptures to
represent humans and some of them "negroid" (God forbid) they declare (4) ancient Egyptians and Nubians were remote in physiognomy
from sub-Saharan negroes and none of them could have been models
for the Negro-looking heads. Finally, fearing they had shot their whole
quiver of arrows into the air, without making their point conclusively
clear, they drop all presence at logic and declare, races are not linked
to noses, jaws nor hair. These are the conclusions of the anthropologists who thought they had proven beyond a doubt that "short, flat
noses are confined to the West African ancestors of African-Americans." Now, cornered by these short, flat noses in their own ancient
backyard, they declare, without a blink of an eyelid, faced with the
horror of their own defensive logic, that (5) "races are not linked to
specific physiognomic traits".[31]

Observe the front of the stone head overleaf. Also, the side of the
head.

It is found in the Olmec world. It is, by all recent dating accounts,
circa 1200 B.C. or later. Look closely at both the front and side of the

(a) **Among the first stone heads found, with Africoid features.** *Front view.* **Tres Zapotes. This was found in 1862. It is now located at Tuxtla.**

(b) *Side view* **of the Tres Zapotes head.**

head and then at the photo that follows on p. 74, the very same head on the back of which dangle seven braids. According to the logic of my critics, this either belongs to a "mythic being" (De la Fuente) or is "the spitting image of a native American" (De Montellano et al) but, God forbid, not the sculpture of a foreign type, and, of all things, not the dreaded Negro.

The darkness of the head with braids and some of the other heads are not distinguishable as Africoid or Negroid simply because of their color. Nowhere on earth is there any head with a combination of braids, a broad, flat, wide-nostrilled nose, very pronounced prognathism, thick, everted lips (even if we ignore the blackness) that a scientist would not classify as African.

The seven braids on the Negroid stone head overleaf is no accident. This phenonenon of seven never appears in ancient America until it refers to ancient visitors (see note 33). It is not just the uniqueness of the braids but the uniqueness of the number seven. It was a sacred number in Egypt and it was to leave its influence on more than one civilization. Wayne Chandler highlights the significance of seven in ancient Egyptian thought and shows how it evolved and how it was to affect other peoples and cultures.

"The great Hermetic Principles or Laws that have been left to us are

(c) Back of the Tres Zapotes head, showing seven braids.

seven in number. *Seven is not just an arbitrary figure, but a powerful and extremely signicant symbol for them of divine and universal cohesiveness.* The following will dramatize this point.

1. "There are seven days in the week and fifty-two weeks in a year (5+2 = 7). The Earth (according to them) was created in six days and on the Seventh Day its Creator rested.

2. They state that Age Seven is the Age of Reason; twice that, Fourteen, is Puberty; thrice that, Twenty One, is Maturation.

3. There are Seven Cardinal Colors in the solar spectrum—violet, indigo, blue, green, yellow, orange, red—from which all other colors are derived.

4. There are Seven Key Notes in the musical scale.

5. They believed at that point in time that there were Seven Continents, Seven Seas, as well as Seven Planets, called the Seven Governors, also referred to as the Seven Angels.

6. There are Seven Holes which lead into the Human Body—ears, nostrils (two in each) mouth, anus, and vaginal or penile orifices. The human brain, heart, eye and ear are each divided into Seven Parts. The skin has Seven Layers.

7. They believed in Seven Virtues and Seven Deadly Sins. To them so many components of human life were connected to expressions of Seven that they thought it sacred."[32]

What makes their emphasis in seven even more significant is that the Egypto-Nubian journey to the Far West of the World in search of a mythical "underworld" (a terrestrial paradise) is documented by both the visitors and the visited and both agree that the journey was made by *seven* ships.

Rafique Jairazbhoy in his book on ancient Egyptians in America (George Prior, London, 1974) presents the Egyptian and native American accounts of this voyage and although they are from other sides of the water, they both agree that seven ships or galleys were involved in this ancient journey and that this (as were the great ships and pyramids they built) was inspired by a religious motive. This is laughable now in our pagan times but these energising myths led to pyramidal constructions that humble even modern technological genius (note details of the failed Japanese attempt to build a pyramid in spite of the advanced technology of the current age.)[33]

"One of the most intriguing questions," writes the Indian scholar, Jairazbhoy, "is the reference to seven ships or galleys". He quotes Father Bernardino de Sahagun as saying that these people came by sea and "it is certain that they came in vessels of wood, but it is not known how they were built; but it is conjectured by a report among the natives, that they came in seven caves, and that these seven caves are the seven ships or galleys. They disembarked at the port of Panuco (north of Veracruz) which they called Panco, which means, "place where those who crossed the water arrived." These people came looking for a terrestrial paradise" (Sahagun, 1946, pp. 13–14; Sorenson, 1955, p. 429). The Popul Vuh, the Bible of the Quiche Maya, has a similar account and they speak of these visitors naming the place where they arrived as "Seven caves, seven canyons" (Popul Vuh, 5259–60).

The account on one side of the water is harmonised by Jairazbhoy with an account on the other. The Americans record seven ships arriving. The Egyptians record seven ships leaving. Both use the symbolic language of the past but the meaning is inescapable for there are paintings of the ships. "In the tomb of Ramses III, there is a room inscribed with the text "Litany of the Sun". The Egyptians believed that there was a terrestrial paradise in the Far West of the World (America) where the sun goeth down and the stars spring up like little suns to relight the darkened room of the world. Thus, in this room of Ramses III (c. 1200 B.C., the first contact period) Jairazbhoy notes there is a ceiling with seven ships among the stars. He cites several authorities for this—Lefebure, M.E.: 1889, pp. 91–92; Champollion: 1945 III, pl.256; Rossellini, J: 1832–44, II, pls. 107, 108)[34]. Even the word for the Egyptian terrestrial paradise "*yaru*" survives in America as "*yaro*" and the word *RA* is also duplicated.

De Montellano claims that *all* the stone heads found in early America are "spitting images of the native American," thereby establishing a reputation for being a world authority on the race-transforming chemistry of ancient spit. As I pointed out at the beginning of this chapter, I am part Macusi Indian. Native Americans dominated my childhood

Figures (a) and (b). Compare (a) *Head of Nuba chief from Kenya* above with (b) *Olmec Negroid stone head (Tres Zapotes F)* (beside it). The one overleaf (p. 77) is "a spitting image of the native American," according to my chief critic, Ortiz de Montellano.

Olmec Negroid Stone Head (Tres Zapotes F). This is "a spitting image of the Native American" (De Montellano et al in *Current Anthropology*).

years. My rivers (the Cuyuni, the Mazaruni, the Essequibo), my mountains (the Roraima, the Pakaraima range), even my lost and beloved country (Guyana—land of waters) were named by them. I also lived in, (*lived* in, not passed through) East Africa, Europe, both East and West, the Americas, both north and south. It puzzles me that a scholar could seriously compare the photo on p. 76 at (a) and the photo beside it at (b) and fail to see even the faintest glimmer of a racial and physiognomic relationship.

Below are two more "spitting images of the native". Do not refer to them as "Negro" or African" (God forbid). My critics say they are just "Negro-looking" and please do not read that to mean they are looking for fellow Negroes. The reason that they have broad noses, full lips, high browridges, etc. is because the tools were "blunt" (Michael Coe) and the reason why they look Black is because most of them were made of "dark volcanic stone" (De Montellano et al.). The ancient carvers, unfortunately, ran out of dark stone and so they made some

Two views of Olmec monument F, Tres Zapotes, Veracruz. Early pre-Classic.

out of white stone which "turned dark over time" (De Montellano et al.). If you are eccentric or Afro-centric and you do not want to accept that one, we quote another expert archeologist who can tell you what they are. They are "half-human, half-jaguar" (Aguirre Beltran). Not yet satisfied? Well, they are "baby faces", not yet fully formed. The *Encyclopedia Brittanica* accepts the last two explanations. But there is more. Beatrice de la Fuente, according to a recent citation by my critics, suggests they are modelled after "mythic beings".

Before we go any further in our display of some of the stone heads of the Olmec period (some of which are undeniably Africoid) I need to explain once again my use of the term "negroid" which does not cover all African phenotypes. It is difficult to avoid this term since one sometimes has to resort to general terms that the majority of readers understand. The Black African, as I demonstrated earlier in this chapter, has at least six variants. All of these African variants have been found, both in the artwork as well as in the tombs and mummy packs of the ancient Egyptian: the Elongated, the Nilotic, the so-called "true Negro", the Bushmanoid or Khoisan, the pygmy, the "Khartoum variant". It is not a matter of "one drop of Black blood makes you Black," to quote a recent simplistic distortion of my position by De Montellano. His ignorance of African phenotypes is understandable and, in the light of our present educational system, excusable, but his Afrophobia or Negrophobia is not. He seems to enjoy parading it like a badge of honor at every turn. When I speak of "the confused racial situation in certain Egyptian dynasties" (a remark quoted in a recent critique of my work) I am speaking of the later invasions that were to lead to intermarriage between invader and invaded and thus alter the face of the Egyptian. That was not the case in 1200 B.C., the first contact period in the time of the Rammesides. We can see this very clearly from the color photograph I have presented of the Egyptian, the Indo-European (or Indo-Aryan), the Nubian and the Semite.

Only the Hyksos invasion (c. 1660 B.C.) the first of half of a dozen invasions, had touched the Egyptian before 1200 B.C. and it left no significant enduring marks, as debates at UNESCO have clearly demonstrated. The invasion of the Assyrian (c. 654 B.C.), the Persian (c. 550 B.C.), the Greek (c. 320 B.C.), the Roman (just before and after Christ), and the Arab (c. A.D. 638–640) were to change the ancient face of the Egyptian and produce such a "confused racial situation" that today there is an attempt by the Arab-dominated government to replace the shattered nose of the Sphinx with an acquiline shape, al-

This unusual photograph of the Sphinx was taken by Dr. Willard Johnson of M.I.T. It should be compared with a startlingly identical line drawing of a facial reconstruction of the Sphinx by New York Detective, Frank Domingo. The drawing, establishing the Africoid features of the Sphinx, appears in a *New York Times* Op-Ed article by John Anthony West.

though Russian skull experts have shown with computerised precision that the nose of the Sphinx is that of the broad Negroid variety. I must point out that I was part of a five–way telephone linkup, along with Dr. Cheikh Anta Diop and Dr. Gamel Abdul Mohktar of UNESCO, in initial negotiations with the British Museum for the return of the splinters of the Sphinx's nose and chin to the Egyptian government. The telephone linkup also included Garland Roberts, who discovered that the British had the pieces, and Jean Paul Boudier, who did translations from the French during this transatlantic dialogue.

The *Encyclopedia Britannica* explains away the Negroid faces of

some of the stone heads as a result of the imaginative marriage of man and jaguar. This "were jaguar" explanation started with another Negrophobic, Aguirre Beltran. Lest some of my readers get locked into this illusion, I present two images of the were jaguar sculptures to show how different they are from the vividly detailed and realistic sculptures of the humans represented in the stone heads.

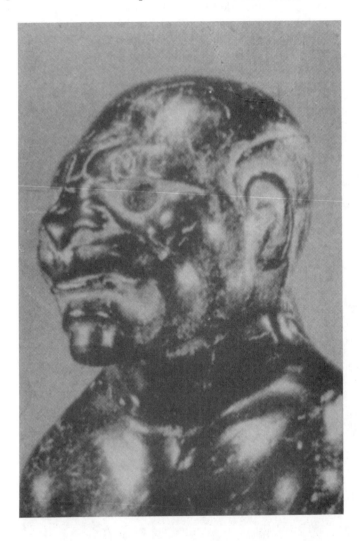

It is important to examine the were-jaguars on p. 81 and 82 and compare them with the head below to see the extremes to which my critics have gone to explain away the realism of the stone heads. Here again they suggest that the sculptor accidentally arrived at "Negro-looking" features because they were trying to blend human with jaguar.

Let us look closely now at parallels between the ancient stone heads we have found in America and those in the Egypto-Nubian world circa 1200 B.C.

Jairazbhoy has provided parallel photographs of stone heads in ancient America and stone heads of Egyptians and Nubians at Tanis in the Egyptian delta circa 1200 B.C. They are startlingly alike in style— *parallel incised lines, flap falling along the side of the face, circular ear plug.* They are also startlingly alike in size. What is more, as Robert Heizer, who is no diffusionist, noted, the heavy transport techniques used in both ancient Egypt and America show "startling identities". Some of the problems confronting the builders in both places involved the transportation of between 2–50 ton blocks of uncut stone from distant quarries, some 60–80 miles away. The transportation of

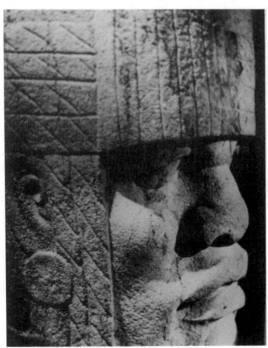

16. Olmec head, San Lorenzo IV. Height 1.78m.

massive stones down the Nile by the Egyptians to the sites where they built their pyramids would daunt even the best of modern engineers. Vast monuments had to be abandoned a few years ago to the rising waters of the Aswan dam because of the difficulty even modern technology faces in moving the colossal monuments of the ancient Egyptians who had devised the most ingenious methods for transporting heavy stones. Why should the methods be startlingly identical (to use Heizer's words) and more than a dozen unique and complex rituals be identical, and the departure and arrival myths identical, and the sound for the terrestrial paradise the Old World party was seeking also be identical (yaru Egyptian, yaro American) and the helmets have the same features, and the features of many of the stone heads match the racial types that then dominated Egypt (before its half a dozen invasions by foriegners)? Is more still needed? Then more shall be given.

One of the African heads in the Olmec world (La Venta) was nine feet high and had its domed head flattened so that it could function as an altar. A hole may be seen at the left ear, running like a tube through the head itself to form a small opening at the center of the mouth. This head was used as an oracle, a "talking god". A priest of the Olmec whispered in that giant ear and his sonorous words emerged from the great stone lips. It is strongly reminiscent of the technique used in the talking god of the Egyptians and Nubians in that ancient time—Amon-Ra. They made Amon-Ra into an animated god. By its oracular pronouncements and the illusion of animation, they could invoke the unchallengeable authority of a god on earth. The statue of Amon-Ra was jointed, a priest being especially appointed to work it, and, in the sanctuaries, hiding places were arranged in the thickness of the wall from which the priest skillfully arranged for the oracular voice of the god to be heard.

Overleaf is a spectacular new stone head found a few years ago. It is staring up at us from the belly of a swamp. Nobody would move it. The federal government of Mexico, I have been made to understand, feels it is the responsibility of the state in which it was found to take care of it. The state feeds it is not their responsibility but that of the federal government. I have sometimes had a secret overwhelming urge to hire a helicopter and lift it out of the swamps under the shadow of night. But this phenomenal thing weighs, as the other stone heads do, at least ten tons. Brood on that fact! For the nearest quarry, rich in this basalt stone, is 60–80 miles downriver and the stone can only be

New head found at San Lorenzo, lying in the swamp.

Africans are still making these colossal stone heads This one was on loan to the Boston Museum, I am told, a few years ago. It was as huge and imposing as some of the ancient stone heads, although (let me make it clear) there is no direct continuity or relationship. It is a contemporary sculpture that stands as high as the first floor of the museum. To use Matthew Stirling's words when he saw the first stone head in America it is "perfect in its proportions . . . amazingly negroid".

transported by water to the ceremonial platform where the other stone heads were found. There is a twenty-two-foot-wide gorge that makes the overland route from the quarry to the place where it was found an impassable nightmare.

Since it was De Montellano et al. who reported in a recent critque that Beatrice de la Fuente suggested that these stone heads were modelled after "mythic beings" I would like to ask (*if that strange report is true*) if these mythic beings or half-human/half-jaguar models had a habit of leaving their skulls and skeletons in the ground, human skulls and skeletons which are "radically different" from the native physical types. I can show a corroboration of the sculptural evidence by an equally meticulous examination of the "human" skeletal remains in the graveyards of the Olmec.

The skeletal evidence at first seemed a problematic proposition since the corrosive humdity of the soil destroyed the bones in the humid capitals of the Olmec. But in the drier centers—Tlatilco, Cerro de las Mesas, and Monte Alban—the Polish craniologist, Andrez Wiercinski, found ample and indisputable evidence of an Africoid presence.

Wiercinski, in 1972, assessed the presence of a negroid pattern of traits on the basis of a multivariate distance analysis of a large set of skull traits which differentiate between Africoid, Mongoloid and Caucasoid varieties. The traits analyzed included "degree of prognathism, prominence of nasal bones, height of nasal roof, width of nasal root, shape of nasal aperture, position of nasal spine, shapes of orbit, depth of canine fossa, and depth of maxillary incisure. [35] Wiercinski sees the colossal heads representing individuals with "negroid" traits predominating but with an admixture of other racial traits. That is what I have said.

The work of A. Vargas Guadarrama is an important reinforcement of Wiercinski's study. Guadarrama's independent analysis of Tlatilco crania revealed that those skulls described by Andrez Wiercinski as "negroid" were *radically different* from the other skulls on the same site. He notes similarities in skull traits between these negroid finds in the Olmec world and finds in West Africa and Egypt. (Wiercinski 1972: 231–252).

What is even more important to note here is that Wiercinski found that 13.5 percent of the skeletons examined in the pre-Classic Olmec cemetery of Tlatilco were Africoid, yet only 4.5 percent of those found at Cerro de las Mesas in the later Classic period were Africoid. [37] This indicates that the African element intermingled until it almost fused with the native population. Female skeletons found in the graves from the pre-Classic period, lying side by side with African males, are racially distinct from them (that is, native American females, foreign African males) but they appear racially similar to their male companions at a later "Classic" site, indicating progressive intermixture and the growing absorption of the foreign African element into the largely Mongoloid American population.

This makes it very clear that the Olmec-African element was a distinctive, outside injection that came and crossbred in the Olmec time period and that it did not represent "proto-Australoid" or "proto-negroid" aborigines who trickled into America from the Pacific in the very ancient epoch when the first Americans came. According to Wiercinski's skeletal statistics, they would have disappeared millennia ago into the American gene pool if they could fade from 13.5 percent to 4.5 percent in a few brief centuries. The two major Pacific migrations of the first Americans occurred, after all, about 50,000 and 20,000 years ago, respectively, according to the most recent datings. (Some have put it as early as 70,000 years ago, others as late as 13,000. In terms of the point I am making—the inevitable fade-out of a distinctive African element if it came in at the very beginning of the Bering Strait migrations—the current dispute over the Bering Strait migration dates does not matter).

In the Olmec civilization, which entered its first distinctive phase circa 1400 B.C. (the first outside contact of Egypto-Nubians occurring circa 1200 B.C.) we are not dealing with proto-negroid elements that survived a Pacific crossing. That is long before the dawn of their civilization (which, by the way, I have never claimed was founded or created by Africans). That is a malicious fabrication by my critics whose tactics seem largely restricted to the invention of straw men to make it easier for their straw brains to knock them down. Contact and influence is the normal intercourse between civilizations, then and now. African civilization made significant contact with a European civilization (A.D. 711-1492) They influenced that civilization in many ways, from medicine to music to mathematics (see detailed documentation of this by European, African, Arab and American scholars)[38] This is not an Afrocentric fantasy. European civilization made its most significant contact with African civilization in 1492 and has significantly influenced Africa unto this day. This is not an Eurocentric fantasy. Contact between civilizations and the influence that flows from contact is natural and inevitable. It was always so. I think even my dumbest critics would agree. Their problem, however, is that they have been numbed and dumbed so profoundly by Negrophobia that they do not believe that any influence can flow from what they consider to be the civilization of jungle bunnies. Hence their infantile and pathetic cry: *not before Columbus*. This has now replaced Mary Leftkowitz's circus slogan: *not out of Africa*.

But the stone heads do not stand by themselves nor do the skulls and skeletons in the graveyards of the Olmec. My critics are equally bewildered by the many terracotta figurines with unmistakable Africoid features. Many absurd explanations have been given to explain why the stone heads are "Negro-looking". I present a few terracotta (overleaf) to add to their probem. Moist heat, they say, accounts for this illusion of an African presence in the terracotta. It accounts, according to them, for black skin, broad noses, kinky hair, prognathism, thick lips, and the unusual goatee beard, a feature so strange on native American chins that when it appeared on an important American personage it was commented upon *ad nauseam* by the European visitors.

My critics claim that "moist heat" accounted for the features overleaf and below.

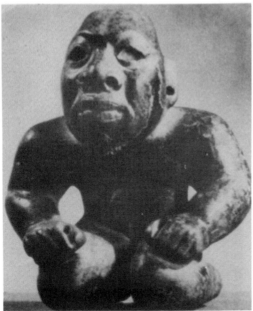

(a) *Late Olmec* **carving from Guatemala. Kneeling figure (jade).**

(b)   (c)   (d)

(b, c, d—Negroid heads in pre-Christian Mexico)
(b) *Guerrero*   **(c)** & **(d)** *Central Plateau of Mexico*

The figures at (b) (c) and (d) had their lips and hair Africanized by moist heat and, in an area where beards were so unusual that, when they occasionally appeared on a native American in the later European contact period, they were heavily commented upon, moist heat sprouted beards on *two of the three chins above.* May I point out here to the trio that I grew up in a native American forest zone in Guyana with moist equatorial heat and never saw these types unless they were a result of intermarriage with Afro-Guyanese.

Pre-classic acrobat. (Photo by Jacqueline Patten-Van Sertima)

Negroid stone head from Vera Cruz, Classic period. **In American Museum of Natural History, New York.**

Negroid head with vivid sacrification. **Vera Cruz.** *Classic* **period. Note headdress.**

Woman from Xochipala. (Photo by Jacqueline Patten-Van Sertima)

With respect to the epicanthic fold in the late Olmec carving on p. 89, it is typical of Afro-Mongoloid mixtures. It is also found in full-blooded Africans. For evidence of Africans with epicanthic fold see Evans-Pritchard and C.G. Seligman in the Sudan and ethnologist C.K. Meek in Northern Nigeria.[39] According to my critics, this is all a result of "moist heat" in the Olmec area.

According to De Montellano, Barbour and Haslip-Viera, the Classic Teotihuacan girl below (right) also displays these Africoid features because of the "moist heat" in that area of Mexico. Moist heat, I suppose, also gave her the distinctive headdress and pendants, apart from the undeniable Africoid combination of nose, lips, black skintone. Fearing this might not go over very well (except with Afrophobics like themselves) they go so far as to suggest that Von Wuthenau, who spent more than a quarter of a century studying and lecturing on art history in Mexico, was probably displaying "forged artifacts". May I point out in defense of the memory of my good friend, that the photo of the African girl on the left is by George Holton, New York, and the

Girl from Nigeria   **Classic Teotihuacan girl**

photo of the Classic Teotihuacan pottery head on the right was taken from Bradley Smith's *History of Art*. (Mexico, 1968). Von Wuthenau juxtaposed them to make it clear to anyone who is not blind or who do not deliberately shut their eyes to avoid seeing the African where the African is "not supposed to be . . . *not before Columbus*" that these are mirror images of each other.[40]

Notes

1. "Golden Age of the Moor" (*Journal of African Civilizations*, vol. 11, 1991 edited by Ivan Van Sertima).
2. See Frontispiece photo in "Golden Age of the Moor" (*JAC*, vol. 11, 1991 African General Boabdil (Abu-abdi-Llah) surrenders to the Spanish (Granada, 1492)
3. De Montellano et al., *Current Anthropology*, 1997 After claiming that native Americans had developed a civilization very early (a view with which I totally agree) they then vilify the native American by suggesting that his early civilization was of such a barbaric order that it encouraged the wanton cannabalism of strangers. All this, on the basis of one isolated instance in the Yucatan, an incident by the way that did not involve Africans. Native Americans greeted the arrival of Africans in their midst on many recorded occasions, even in some instances according them the high honor of chiefdoms (see *The Red and the Black* by Lorenz Katz.)
4. *They Came Before Columbus*, p. 147
5. *Journal of African Civilizations*, vol. 8, no. 2, 1986, p.16
6. De Montellano et al, *Current Anthropology*, 1997. It should be noted that I was invited to respond to the critique but when I did so I was originally only allowed 800 words as against 55 pages by my trio of critics. Eventually, under the pressure of my protest, I was conceded 15 pages. When I sought permission to reprint this 15 page response to the slanders and misrepresentations, the editor wrote me saying that, once I signed the agreement to let them publish my 15 pages, I no longer had rights to republish my own initial response (forced by their rules to be as brief as possible) *unless* I republished the whole book of their misrepresentations and slanders "since they form a unit".
7. The four books I have edited and published on the race, culture and science of the ancient Egyptians are:
   1. *Nile Valley Civilizations* (1985)
   2. *Great African Thinkers* (1986)
   3. *Egypt Revisited* (1989)
   4. *Egypt: Child of Africa* (1994)
   (All the volumes, except *Nile Valley Civilizations*, are still in print).
8. Keith Crawford, "Racial Identity of Egyptian Populations based on the Analysis of Physical Remains", *Journal of African Civilizations*, vol. 12, p. 55ff.
9. Dana Reynolds-Marniche, "The Myth of the Mediterranean Race" in *Journal of African Civilizations*, vol. 12, 1995:105–125.
10. Keith Crawford, *JAC*, vol. 12, 1995, p. 61.
11. Runoko Rashidi, *JAC*, vol. 12, p. 105–107.
12. "Earliest Monarchy Found in Nubia", *New York Times*, March 1, 1979, A1.
13. Bruce Williams, "The Lost Pharaohs of Nubia," *Archeology Magazine*, vol. 33, no. 5. Reprinted in J.A.C. vol. 10, 1989, p. 90–104

14. Timothy Kendall, *Meroitica*, 1996. Cites 16 Nubian Pharaohs who preceded the 25th dynasty.
15. Wayne Chandler, "Of Gods and Men: Egypt's Old Kingdom", *Journal of African Civilizations*, vol. 10, 1989, p. 117–182.
16. *Historia de los Cosas de Nueva España*, Mexico, 1829.
17. *Egypt Revisited, Journal of African Civilizations*, Vol. 10, 1989, p. 27.
18. G. A. Wainwright in *Man*, October, 1951, p. 133–135 (ancient Egyptian breast-plate found in ancient context in Lagos, Nigeria)
19. Lady Lugard, *A Tropical Dependency*, chapter 26, London, 1905. Recently re-printed by Black Classic Press (evidence of ancient Egyptian contact with, and influence on, the Hausa).
20. Hunter Adams, "African Observers of the Universe: The Sirius Question." *Journal of African Civilizations*, vol. 5, 1983, p. 27–46.
21. Cheihk Anta Diop, "Origin of the Ancient Egyptians" in *Journal of African Civilizations*, vol. 10, p. 9–38 (Quotation p. 23–26).
22. James Bailey, *The God Kings and the Titans*, St. Martin's Press, New York, 1973, p. 87.
23. G. Elliot Smith, "Ships as Evidence of the Migration of Early Cultures", *Journal of the Manchester Egyptian and Oriental Society*, 1916, pp. 63–102. Readers should note that this quotation from Elliot Smith deals specifically with a com-parative study of ancient ships—their oars, rudders, masts, sails, hulls, transverse beams, mat-covered cabins. These comparisons have been closely examined by other experts in this field and are not in question. I go to great pains to point this out, that these are closely examined and unquestioned comparisons. I do not share the hyper-diffusionist views of Elliot Smith who believed that all civilizations sprang from some single source.
24. Runoko Rashidi, "Royal Ships of the Pharaohs", *Journal of African Civilizations*, vol. 12, 1994.
25. Matthew W. Stirling, "Discovering the New World's Oldest Dated Work of Man," *National Geographic Magazine*, vol. 76 (August, 1939) pp. 183–218.
26. Beatrice de la Fuente, *Las Cabezas Colosales Olmeca* (reference lost but I quote her, as translated from the Spanish) "If in some moment one appeared to ponder on the existence of Negroes in [early] Mesoamerica, such a thought would surely occur after you have seen the head at Tres Zapotes (Tres Zapotes 2) the most remote in physiognomy from our indigenous ancestors. The elevated position of this personage is revealed in the headdress from which dangles seven bands which figure braids that taper off into rings and tassels." Of course, like Frederick Peterson, who spokes of "a strong Negroid substratum connected with the Olmec magicians" she later backed down from her first impressions. They all bowed to the ruling wisdom of their Negrophobic colleagues. They are not to be dismissed for this. They are otherwise sound scholars and honorable men and women. We have all been affected by the frozen attitudes of our time. It takes a great deal of courage and, sometimes, a bit of downright foolhardiness, to maintain and pursue an antiestablishment position.
27. Dr. Clarence Weiant, *New York Times* (Letters) May 1, 1977.
28. *Current Anthropology*, June, 1997
29. Cited in a recent attack by de Montellano et al. This remark, they claimed, was made by "de la Fuente, 1992, p. 130–133".
30. *Readers' Digest*, 1986, p. 140
31. *Current Anthropology*—June 1997. This was sent to me in an unpublished form

but the editor, Richard Fox (after I refused to permit publication of my response *if it meant losing my rights to my own work*) issued a statement to the effect that I had withdrawn from the debate and never sent me the final published version. Whether they cleaned up some of their racist remarks after my unpublished counter-attack, it is important that the public should know the extent to which this trio would go in their Negrophobic rage to cancel out the role of the African in history.

32. Wayne Chandler, "Seven Times Seven: The Seven Hermetic Principles of Ancient Egypt", *Journal of African Civilizations*, vol. 12, 1995, p. 214–229.
33. *Egypt Revisited*, Vol 10, 1989, p. 145–153.
34. Jairazbhoy, *Ancient Egyptians and Chinese in America*, George Prior Associated Publishers, London 1974.
35. *Current Anthropology*, op. cit.
36. Andrez Wiercinski, 1972 "Inter and Interpopulational Racial Differentiation of Tlatilco, Cerro de las Mesas, Monte Alban and Yucatan Maya" in the Thirty-ninth Congresso Internacional de Americanistas, Actas y Memorias, Vol. 1, Lima.
37. Ibid.
38. Ibid.
39. Ivan Van Sertima, editor, *Golden Age of the Moor*, Vol. 11, Journal of African Civilizations, Fall, 1991.
40. (a) C.K. Meek, 1931, *A Sudanese Kingdom.* London: Kegan Paul, Trench Trubner
    (b) Charles G. Seligman, 1932, *Pagan Tribes of the Nilotic Sudan.* London: Routledge and Kegan Paul.
41. Alexander Von Wuthenau, *Unexpected Faces in Ancient America.*

Ritual Correspondences

But evidence of a physical presence is only half of the story. What influence did these outsiders have, if any, on the native? Before I answer that question I want to make it clear once again that any contact between two peoples and cultures can lead to a cross-fertilization; and that to find a dozen or even a score amid a hundred and one elements in a civilization that strongly suggest borrowing, does not negate a native originality nor an indigenous base for the civilization. Nor does it necessarily constitute a claim that the outsider is superior to the native. In fact, there are instances in history in which the invader was more affected by the civilization of the invaded than vice versa. A classic example of this, though still unacknowledged, is the impact on the culture of the conquering Greeks by the conquered Egyptian.

There are ritual parallels between the Olmec and the Egyptian that are so startling that they bear serious examination, especially in the light of visible evidence of a physical presence. All sorts of claims have been made by diffusionists, but the few I shall present here meet rigorous criteria: (1) traits that appear in an interrelated cluster rather than single-trait correspondences; (2) traits that are unique to the two culture areas, in that they appear nowhere else in the world save where they can be shown to have diffused from what we claim to be the outsider or donor culture; (3) traits that are so complex or arbitrary that it is remotely unlikely that they should occur in the same form and with the same function in cultures far apart; and (4) traits for which there is abundant evidence of antecedence in the donor culture and no such known evidence at the moment in the supposed recipient.

Consider, first, half a dozen or so monarchic traits—traits associated with the priest-caste or ruling elite of both civilizations. One such trait is the use of purple as an index of royal or noble rank. The religious value of purple and its use to distinguish priests and people of high rank is well known among the dynastic Egyptians. What is little known, however, is that its use grew out of unique circumstances and is found nowhere in the Old World save where it can be shown to have diffused from its original center. Sanctity was attached to shell purple because the murex shell from which it was extracted changed color in the same way as the Nile in flood. The Egyptians therefore considered purple a noble and sacred color, and, through the Phoenicians, who adopted the purple industry, the association of purple with royalty, the priesthood, and the high-born, spread throughout the Mediterranean[1] (Van Sertima; see also Mackenzie[2]).

We find purple having the same value in the Olmec world. Both Matthew Stirling and Medellin Zenil noted that a patch of purple appears on one of the monumental stone heads at San Lorenzo. In fact, Medellin Zenil[3] claims that some of the heads were originally painted purple but that *the paint faded over time*. In the Nuttall Codex, Zelia Nuttall, the discoverer of the codex, notes "pictures of no fewer than thirteen Mexican women of rank wearing purple skirts and five with capes and jackets of the same color. In addition, forty-five chieftains are figured with short, fringed, round purple waistcloths, and there are also three examples of the use of a close fitting purple cap."[4]

It is natural that the original purple would fade to a reddish hue in some places due to weathering and the passage of time. This critical detail has escaped my amateurish critics who, without careful examination and, in their indecent haste to debunk me, have recently claimed in their series *Not Before Columbus* (mimicking Leftkowitz's *Not Out of Africa*) that Zenil and Medellin were mistaking red for purple, that the Americans never used purple. Their scholarship and their respect for professional objectivity, even in the heat of debate, does not seem to have improved with time. They turn *purple* with justifiable rage (no one likes to be defeated in public debate) but then they simmer down to a raw rude *red*, blushing under the blast of a hundred truths, truths which can only appear for a while to be sullied by deceptions, deceptions which they should learn are extremely dangerous, since, the more daring and dirty they are, the more easily and certainly will they eventually be exposed as lies.

Olmec dignitary at Cerro de la Piedra wearing double crown. Museo Nacional, Mexico City. Courtesy R. A. Jairazbhoy

The figure above depicts an Olmec dignitary at Cierro de la Piedra. This is clearly a Native American. He is probably a king and he has one of his subjects bound and seated at his feet. Upon this royal head stands something thus far found in only two culture areas of the world:

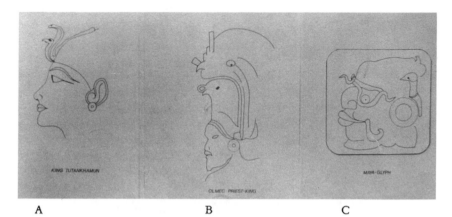

A   B   C

a. Bird and serpent on the crown of the boy-king Tutankh-amun. b. Bird and serpent on another Olmec dignitary. c. Bird and serpent on the crown of a Mayan chief. Courtesy R. A. Jairazbhoy

the double crown. The double crown in the Egypto-Nubian world grew out of special historical circumstances. It signified the joining of the two lands, the north and south, Egypt and Nubia. Even more unusual is the bird and serpent motif on royal diadems and crowns. Yet here, in this extraordinary glimpse of an Olmec king, we see the duplication of not one, but two, indisputably unique traits. Not just the double crown, but the lower crown with the head of a serpent and the upper crown with the head of a bird.

It would surely be impossible to find such a mirrored duplication of a complex and arbitrarily fused twin trait in any other cultural context, in any other historical period, in any other part of the world, without some demonstrable evidence of contact between the mother of the original trait and its duplicate.

The figure above shows the bird and serpent on the crown of the boy-king Tutankhamen, son of the Nubian queen, Tiye. This is again shown on the head of yet another Olmec dignitary in figure b, and on the head of a Mayan Chief in figure c, to whom it diffused from the Olmec high-culture.

There is the royal crook and the royal flail, part of the ceremonial regalia of priest-kings in both areas. Jairazbhoy[5] (1974:21, illustr. 15) mentions an Olmec painting at Oxtotitlan in which the Olmec king seated on the throne has the same type of flail as the Egyptian, and it is in the same position behind his head. But this interconnected cluster of monarchic traits also contains the sacred boat or ceremonial bark of the priest-kings. What is so remarkable about this is that it not only has the same function but the same sound: *sibak* in Egyptian, *cipac* in Mexican (the *b* and *p*, of course, are interchangeable plosives).

In an earlier work, I noted that the parasol or ceremonial umbrella was reserved for royalty in both civilizations. It is actually recorded in Mexican tradition as having come across the water from the east by way of foreigners. Jairazbhoy mentions this little known oral tradition recorded in the Titulo Coyoi, one of the surviving texts of the Quiche Maya, influenced by the ancient Olmec. The tradition harks back to early visitors. "These things came from the east," it says, "from the other side of the water and the sea: they came here, they had their throne, their little benches and stools, they had their parasols and their bone flutes"[6] (Jairazbhoy 1974:10).

Jairazbhoy also draws our attention to another unusual monarchic trait duplicated in the Olmec world—feathered fans used by Egyptian royalty that are almost identical in shape, style, and color to royal fans found in ancient Mexican paintings in the pyramid of Las Higueras. These fans were painted in an area once dominated by the Olmec and in a culture clearly influenced by them, even though the culture itself (Totonac) belongs to a slightly later period. The fans are made of feathers arranged in concentric circles of blue, red, and green. In Mexico they are blue, red, and light blue, but the Mexican light blue is the nearest thing on the color spectrum to the Egyptian green.. Further unique parallels and identities can be found in some of their ritual ceremonies and ceremonial objects. Individually, some of these traits might be dismissed as coincidence. The density of the cluster, however, the range and extent of the duplication, with very minor local variations—especially in the light of what we have seen of the iconographic and skeletal evidence—cancels out such a simplistic explanation. As I have said in an earlier work, "The overwhelming incidence of coincidence argues overwhelmingly against a mere coincidence."

The ceremony depicted in the figure overleaf reveals another combination of near-identities. The Egyptian papyrus painting (overleaf) is taken from the Book of the Dead. It depicts the Opening of the Mouth ceremony. Compare it with the wall painting beside it from a cave at Juxtlahuaca. The priests in Mexico and Egypt are wearing the skins of beasts, whose heads cover theirs, like masks, and whose tails hang in the identical manner between their legs. They both proffer a snake-headed wand or stick, as well as another object (unidentifiable but similar) to a bearded, seated figure before them[7] (Jairazbhoy 1974:25).

(a) Opening of the Mouth ceremony from the Egyptian Book of the Dead
(b) Wall painting from a cave at Juxtlahuaca
Courtesy R.A. Jairazbhoy

In Egypt the Pharaoh is purified by the gods Thoth and Horus, pouring crossed streams of libation over him (figure A). In the Mexican Codex we see the same ceremony (figure B). Here are two underworld gods pouring crossed streams of libation over a third god (Jairazbhoy 1974: 44, illustr. 27).[8]

Egyptian   **Olmec**

Egyptian libation scene with Pharaoh   Scene from Mexican Codex with
purified by the gods Thoth and Horus.   crossed streams of libation
Notice crossed streams.   poured by two Underworld gods
                                             over another.

Among the most startling of identities between the two cultures because they are found nowhere else in that phase of time is the human-headed bird, the Ba and Ka[9] (Jairazhbhoy 1974:81). The figure below provides a comparison in ancient Egypt. These human-headed birds are found on sarcophagi in both Egypt and Mexico, and holes are cut in the tombs in both places so that the soul of the deceased, which it represents, can come and go. The jackal-headed human, Anubis, is another common feature. I have seen it in the museum of Villahermosa, which houses many of the treasures of ancient La Venta. (I was not allowed to photograph it.)

a. Human-headed bird in ancient America. b. Human-headed bird in ancient Egypt. Courtesy R. A. Jairazhboy

a   b

Another remarkable pair of human-headed objects appears in figures below. The one on the left is from early America, Costa Rica, with a very realistic African head at one end and a penis with two stylized footrests at the other. The one on the right—a human-headed coffin from Argin in ancient Nubia—has African features like the American one on the left, spectacularly sculpted into the funerary wood.

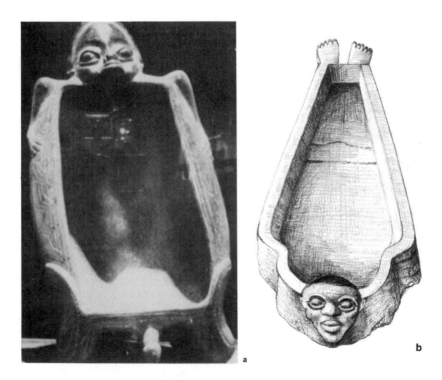

Figure a. Human-headed coffin from pre-Columbian Costa Rica.
b. Human-headed coffin from Argin in Nubia. Courtesy Alexander von Wuthenau

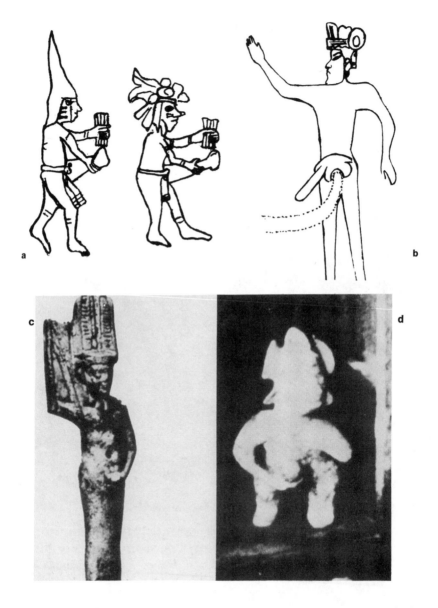

Phallic cults in Egypt and Mexico: (a) Phallic procession in Mexican Codex Borbonicus holding artificial phalli; (b) Olmec painting of phallic figure from Oxtotitlan with right arm upraised; (c) Egyptian god Min from Medinet Habu holding phallus and raising right hand; (d) Mexican terracotta figure with man holding phallus in the manner of the Egyptian god Min.

Jairazbhoy demonstrates the remarkable similarity between several gods in the Egyptian underworld and early Mexico. Two that are particularly convincing are the god Sokar (at A) and the god at Izapa in Mexico (at B). Sokar is a winged god who stands on the back of a double-headed serpent.[10] He stretches out his hand to hold up his wings. The Mexican god does the same. He also stands on the back of a serpent who has the same unique mythological form—a head where his head should be, as well as a head where his tail should be.

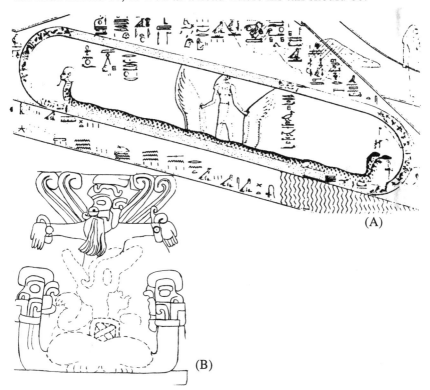

(A)

(B)

Certainly unusual in the ritual of the ancient world was the plucking out of the human heart. There is a representation of it in Egypt (see overleaf).[11] Here, the enemies of the sun-god have their hearts plucked out. This was simply symbolic in Egypt but it became terrifyingly real in Mexico, where human hearts (often from the breasts of subject tribes) were torn out and fed to the sun-god. It can be argued, however, that the idea blossomed independently, by sheer coincidence, among these two peoples and cultures, although one would be hard put to show its parallel elsewhere in the ancient world.

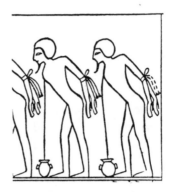

Egyptian representation of the enemies of the sun god with their hearts plucked out in the Underworld. Compare the Mexican Underworld with the heart being devoured, and the Mexican human sacrifice in which the heart was plucked out and offered to the sun.

"A single culture element found to appear at both ends of a natural sea route," wrote Heyerdahl, "may very well be the result of coincidence or independent evolution along parallel lines. To become a reasonable indicator of contact, a whole array of identities or similarities of extraordinary nature must be concentrated in the two areas linked by a land bridge or *marine conveyor belt*.

. . . What confronts us . . . on both side of the Atlantic are arrays of cultural parallels and when these are dealt with as complexes, we are faced by amazing statistical indications . . . When the whole list of parallels are considered together as an entity then the probability of diffusion rather than independent development does not increase arithmetically but exponentially; for instance, a cluster of twelve parallels grouped together does not weigh twelve times heavier in the discussion than a single parallel, but rather, according to the laws of probability, has increased its significance by a truly astronomical amount. Among other things, this means that the Isolationist's technique of negating these parallels one by one by labeling them 'coincidence' is mathematically invalid."[12]

Jairazbhoy presents several more, more than the dozen complex and unique identicals which Heyerdahl suggests would be "astronomical" and double the eight that science now considers as clearly indicative of a contact and an influence. Those I present here are the ones I selected from Jairazbhoy's work for use in my address to the Smithsonian (1991). The human-headed coffin on page 105 is my Nubian selection from Von Wuthenau's "Unexpected Faces".

De Montellano et al. have carefully avoided challenging all but *one* of the ritual correspondences (the royal use of purple) in their coordinated and well-financed attack on my thesis. Although all the conservative magazines are open to them but closed to me, they use this opportunity simply to set up straw men in order to knock them down with what appears to be apparent ease, but is really amateurish expertise. They have descended into brazen attempts not only at fabricating what I said but even fabricating the dating of the stone heads.

They claim, for example, that, on the basis of stratigraphic associations, 16 Olmec monuments have been placed in the final stages of the San Lorenzo B stage (1011 B.C.) and therefore cannot be younger than 1011 B.C. They also state that Ann Cyphers radio-carbon dated the undisturbed context of *one* head (note, *one isolated head*) and found it to be a bit earlier than 1011 B.C. They then admit that "it is impossible to unequivocally date all the heads" but that this isolated head (just a bit earlier than 1011 B.C.) *proves* that "Negro-looking heads were being carved, mutilated and buried prior to 1200 B.C." This is patently absurd for even if, for the sake of argument, the first San Lorenzo stage were centuries earlier, that would not prove that at the birth of the culture itself giant stone heads were being carved, mutilated and buried, all in one joint creative and destructive huff, circa 1200 B.C. and then, in a later and less murderous mood (c. 1011 B.C.) recarved. Is this said out of frustration at them finding they cannot "unequivocally date the heads"? Are they assuming also, to safeguard their shaky case, that as soon as the native American started his civilization he put all the elements into place and by 1200 B.C. he was tearing it all down, mutilating it so badly and burying it with such great rage that centuries after (1011 B.C.) he felt such a twinge of regret at wanton destruction of his heritage that he started penitently resculpturing the heads? Let me remind them also, lest they start playing with the dates, that new evidence now emerging (see part 3) show South American cocaine turning up in Egypt in the belly of Ramses II (which is earlier than 1200 B.C.)

We have made no claim that African-Egyptians and African-Nubians founded and created American civilization. A civilization is made up of many pieces. No civilization makes contact with any other civilization without one of them exerting some influence on the other. This is not always visible in *both* the visitor and the visited. It is dependent on a lot of factors. Outside of physical evidence, which would have been acceptable if it did not involve the dreaded Negro, I have provided a range of ritual parallels that meet all the criteria that science demands in such a case—uniqueness, complexity, clear evidence of antecedence. But my critics accuse me of claiming that Africans were "superior" and Americans "inferior" and that I said Africans "founded" native American civilization. To show how out of touch they are with the native American whom they pretend to defend, they scandalously suggest at one point that these people *as much my people as the African people*, would have "sacrificed and eaten Africans if they came." I present a photograph of two Native American chiefs sitting beside an African chief. This African was not only accepted by them but became one of them and, if being made a chief, is, in the eyes of my critics, what cannibals do to the people who they are about to eat, then God help the state of current anthropology.

This remarkable photo of native American chiefs sitting with an African chief (from *The Red and the Black* by Lorenz Katz, published by Simon and Schuster, New York) gives the lie to the statement of my critics in *Current Anthropology* that "native Americans would have sacrificed and eaten Africans if they came."

Attempts to manufacture dates for the carving, mutilation, and burial of the Olmec stone heads, after frankly admitting that "we cannot unequivocally date the heads" brings to mind the attempt by an American archeological team to alter the appearance of a figure found with a nose-ball. The nose was recarved and made to look acquiline and the ancient sculpture was dubbed with the appelation, *Uncle Sam.* The figure below shows what it looked like when it was originally found. Note overleaf the dramatic reconstruction of the stone carving.

Before (with ball on nose)

The large bulbous nose has been recut. It has actually been made to look aquiline. Once again, in the face of an apparent deception, we are called upon to be gracious. The nose, we must assume, appeared too big, too broad, too bulbous to be real. How could the discoverers not but conclude that vandals or the blows of time had enlarged it? So what were they expected to do to restore this ancient personage to its original dignity? Why, history had already suggested the perfect solution. The huge African nose on ancient royal sculpture had led Napoleon's army to shoot off its cannon. Later invaders were to fracture and flatten this nose, shatter and splinter it. But these good gentlemen went one step further. They filed it down to fit in with their fancy or fantasy of what it should be. They resculptured the objectionable protuberance. They "refined" it.

After (ball on nose removed)
Figured altered by discoverers, later labelled "Uncle Sam"

Notes

1. Ivan Van Sertima, *They Came Before Columbus*, 1976, p. 165–167
2. Donald McKenzie, *Myths of Pre-Columbian America*, London: Gresham 1924, p. 303, 305, 307.
3. Medellin Alfonso Zenil, *Monolitos Ineditos Olmecas*, 1960, University of Vera Cruz
4. McKenzie, 1924, p. 303
5. Jairazbhoy, *Ancient Egyptians and Chinese in America*, London, Karnak House 1974, p. 21, illustration 15 (royal crook and royal flail).
6. Jairazbhoy, Ibid, p. 10. (throne, royal benches and stools, parasols, bone flutes).
7. Ibid, p. 25 (opening the mouth ceremony).
8. Ibid. p.44, illustration 27 (pouring crossed streams).
9. Ibid. p.108, illustration 86/87 (human-headed birds).
10. Ibid. p. 61, Illustration 60 (winged-god Sokar on double-headed serpent).
11. Ibid. p. 69, illustration 69 (plucking out the heart to feed the sun god).
12. Thor Heyerdahl in Gordon Ashe (ed.) *The Quest for America*, New York, Praeger Publishers, 1971, p. 230

3

Egyptian Contact with South America

Six years ago (in 1992) researchers in Munich began to investigate the contents of ancient Egyptian mummies. As part of this study, they wanted to test for drugs and so they called in a toxicologist, Dr. Balabanova, for help. Dr. Balabanova, of the Institute of Forensic Medicine, Ulm, had developed new methods for detecting drugs in hair. She was so highly respected in this field that police even in the United States use her method to test suspected drug users. Her infallible test for drugs turned up startling results when she tested these Egyptian mummies in Munich. The results were so startling that even she, to use her own words, was "absolutely sure it must be a mistake". She not only ran the tests again to make sure but she sent fresh samples to three other labs. The results were the same. No mistake. The drugs she had detected were certainly there. The discovery caused a furor. Nicotine and cocaine in ancient Egypt? Nonsense! Utterly impossible! Not outside America. Not in ancient times. *Not before Columbus.*

"I got a pile of letters," she complained, "that were almost threatening, insulting, saying it was nonsense, that I was fantasizing, that it was impossible, because it was proven that before Columbus these plants were not found anywhere in the world outside of the Americas."

I pointed out in 1979 in a letter to Dr. Diop, then head of the Radiocarbon laboratory in Dakar, the only African who was allowed to see and examine the ancient mummy of Ramses II, that the *nicotine* found in that ancient mummy was *not necessarily American* in origin. (see chapter 4, Reply to My Critics) Recent studies have borne me out. The few ancient corpses examined in China, Germany, Austria, Egypt and the Sudan do show the presence of nicotine. But the argument I presented to Diop, (after a long study of smoking, tobacco and pipes) advanced the case for an independent Old World/New World nicotine. *Not so cocaine!* Cocaine is a very different matter.

Dr. John Henry, a consultant toxicologoist of Guys Hospital in London, suggested that "probably there is contamination present. Maybe there's a fraud of some kind". But Dr. Balabanova had checked all the lab equipment for contamination. She was so anxious to ensure that the tests on the mummies were beyond question that she used the technique police use in the United States to trap drug users—*the hair-shaft test*. Drugs and other substances consumed by humans get into the hair protein, where they stay forever—even after death. Corpses may eventually break up and dissolve over the centuries. But the dynastic Egyptians embalmed, and so preserved for millenia, their kings and queens and nobles. Thus we can apply the "hair shaft test" even in this late day. Dr. Henry himself, in spite of his initial doubts, made it clear that the hair shaft test is fully accepted and indisputable, "If you know you've taken your hair sample from an individual and the hair shaft is known to contain a drug, then it is proof positive that the person has taken that drug, It is accepted in law. It puts people in prison".

Since the fault could not be found in the tests and no one would be willing to believe that cocaine could find its way into Egypt before Columbus had deflowered the virgin Atlantic, an original explanation that would not shatter the time-honored myth of the discoverer had to be concocted. Alas, this proved to be a dangerous and potentially expensive explanation: *The mummies tested in the museums by Balabanova must all be fake!*

Rosalie David, Keeper of Egyptology in the Manchester Museum, faced with the menacing validity of the hair-shaft test, suggested fakes—the only other possible explanation that could preserve the Columbus myth. "Possibly the mummies that have been tested were not truly ancient Egyptian. They could be false, relatively modern mummies. Traces of cocaine could have turned up in these fakes."

Now it is true that there was a trade in some fake mummies in Victorian times and even after. So Rosalie David decided to check out her theory about "fakes."

As I said at the beginning Balabanova had tested seven mummies from the Munich museum and so Rosalie David went to Munich to follow up on her hunch. Inside the museum she found the sarcophagus of Anut Tawi—the Lady of the Two Lands. She discovered from the museum catalogue that the coffin was bought by King Ludwig from an English traveller called Dodwell in 1845. Anut Tawi was said to have come from a tomb reserved for the priests and priestesses of the god Amun at Thebes. I present a photo of an ancient mummy *answering to this very name* (see overleaf). *This one is in the Cairo Museum, not from Munich.* Rosalie David was never shown the mummy itself but only the sarcophagus in which it lay. Dr. Alfred Grimm, curator of the Egyptian Museum in Munich, afraid that Babalanova's tests on the Munich mummies had already started an embarassing controversy, would not let David see any of the mummies. "Investigations show that the Munich mummies are real Egyptian mummies, no fakes, no modern mummies." he said. "They definitely come from ancient Egypt. But we cannot show them to you. On grounds of religious respect we don't show these mummies here in our galleries. Furthermore, we don't allow anyone to film the mummies and to show them on TV."

He was obviously ill at ease and had abruptly changed the museum rules. The mummies had already been shown on TV before Balabanova found the cocaine. But her discovery, upsetting the conventional wisdom that America had never been visited in ancient times, had caused quite a fuss. The museum wanted nothing more to do with that. That type of research, the curator pointed out, was "far from respectable". In fact "it's not *absolutely* proven and it's not *absolutely* scientifically correct".

But Rosalie David persisted. It was not necessary after all to see and test the mummies. Balabanova had already done so. What she needed was proof that they were genuine. Speaking with the care and caution of a diplomat, knowing how many old fogies would be upset, she made this statement.

"From the documentation and the research which has been carried out on the Munich mummies it seems evident that they are probably genuine because they have packages of viscera inside, some with wax images of the gods on them. Also the state of mummification is very good. I can't comment on those that were only detached heads but the complete bodies strike me as genuine."

But the result from the Munich mummies was not the only evidence from the dead. Balabanova tested tissue from 134 preserved bodies from an excavated cemetery in the Sudan when it was part of the

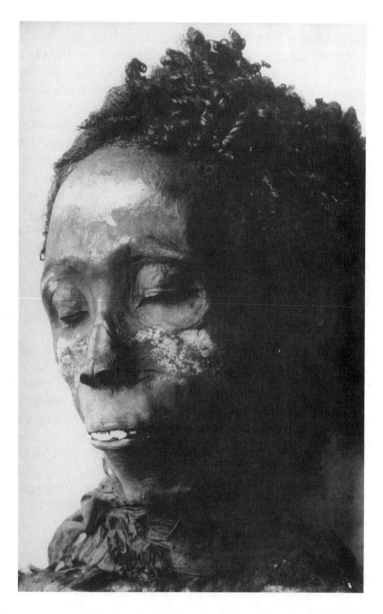

Mummy of an "Anut Tawi" (Cairo Museum) approximately 3,200 years old. This is *not* the Anut Tawi in the Munich Museum, in whose mummified body Dr. Balabanova found cocaine. Rosalie David of the Manchester Museum was not allowed to see or photograph the Munich Anut Tawi, in whose body they found American cocaine.

ancient Egyptian empire. They belonged to a period many centuries before Columbus. They tested positive for both nicotine and cocaine. She thought she might have a way of explaining the nicotine (I did that in my 1979 letter to Diop[1] (see chapter 4, Reply to My Critics) when the international team, of which he was a part, was startled by the presence of the nicotine, (so startled in fact that they abandoned study of the mummy and circulated a rumor that it was not really the mummy of Ramses II at all). But—and this is the crux of the matter—she remained utterly mystified by the cocaine. This could not be explained away. This was definitely *not* indigenous to Africa. A check on all the drug plants outside of America was made—nicotine, mandrake, cannabis, opium, hashish, the lotus flower. *But not cocaine.* This was clearly and undeniably American.

It is important to note that, while a thorough study was done by many authorities, so startled they were by these finds, no one, not a single botanist, believed in a disappearing African coca plant. There is absolutely no evidence of it in the African family of plants. There are actually species of the coca family which grew in *Africa but only the South American species has ever been shown to contain the drug.*

"It's completely unclear," says Balabanova "how cocaine got into Africa. But it's conceivable that the coca plant had been imported into Egypt even then." This is a reluctant but honest admission that the world was not separated by its great waters until Columbus came.

The Internet exchanges over the find of South American cocaine in ancient mummies is most revealing of the racial prejudices which still overshadow serious scholarship today.

It was seriously suggested, since it is now becoming difficult to challenge the fact that the ancient Egyptians (before the five major invasions) were predominantly African, that perhaps the Chinese sailed all the way to America to obtain the cocaine so that they could use it in a trade with Egypt.

Just imagine that! No cocaine has been found so far in any Chinese mummy (Chinese mummification by the way was later than that of Egypt) and no trade links, as far as I know, have yet been established between China and Egypt. Nor do the Chinese have a map of South America or any of the two oceans abutting the Americas whereas the Egyptians had an ancient map (the Piri Re'is map) which shows details of both the western coast of Africa, the Atlantic Ocean, and the eastern coast of South America with some astonishing details that were not known even 200 years after Columbus. But, according to some of the Negrophobic professors on the Internet, perhaps the Chinese did it. Thank God for that way out, since recent studies of the ancient races of Egypt show that we would have to deal with Africans upsetting our favorite Father Chris Columbus myth.

The Internet exchange went even further than that. Several professors were called up to give their one-item proofs that everybody was crossing the ocean except the Africans. A few peanuts in China was accepted as proof that the Chinese were there. A few sculptures of goddesses found in India, holding in their hands a few sculptures of what appear to be maize-cobs, were accepted as proof that the Indians were there. A few Roman jars were accepted as proof that the Romans were there. But:

1. more than a dozen stone heads, some of which were indisputably African in physiognomy;
2. scores of skulls and skeletons of a non-native type found by skeletal experts in the dry areas of the Olmec world, at Tlatilco, Cerro de las Mesas and Monte Alban;
3. an impressive range of terracotta figurines representing African types in all their particulars (hair texture, distinctive African coiffures and earrings, beards, lips, noses, color of skin);
4. a dozen and more unique and complex Egypto-Nubian rituals with clear antecedence in the Old World, duplicated in startling detail in areas where "amazingly Negroid" stone heads, terracotta figurines, Negroid skulls and skeletons, have been found;
5. a tell-tale dwindling in percentage of the foriegn Africoid type found in the Olmec graveyards, dwindling slowly from 13.5 to 4.5 in a few generations as proof that they were *not* the original native but were slowly being absorbed by inter-marriage, into the gene pool of the native American;
6. an ancient Egyptian map of the western outlines of Africa and the eastern seaboard of South America, which, while carrying a few later added details as it was redrawn, places its meridian in Egypt and includes astonishing details (correct latitudinal and longitudinal coordinates between the two continents, the island of Marajo, the true course of the Amazon, etc.) details totally unknown to Europeans about two centuries after Columbus (see Charles Finch's detailed response and excerpts from Covey's study in this section, exposing a mendacious distortion of the facts by my critics concerning this map); and
7. reports by Rafique Jairazbhoy of Egyptian heiroglyphs found in a pre-Columbian context at Portrero Nuevo.

All of the above and yet the Africans could not possibly have been here until the world's "senior" races were here. In the words of Dr. Grimm of the Munich Museum, who refused Rosalie David permission to view Egyptian mummies after American cocaine was found in them: "Such a theory (of an Afro-Egyptian presence in the New World) cannot be entertained by respectable scholars. It is overall absurd."

The most remarkable piece of evidence that Egyptians had travelled to South America lies in the Piri Re'is map, which was *redrawn* around 300 B.C. but belongs to an even earlier period. This ancient Egyptian map shows the relatively correct latitudinal and and longitudinal coordinates between the Atlantic coasts of Africa and South America.

This map shows beyond the shadow of a doubt that Africans crossed the Atlantic in pre-Christian times. It is indisputably pre-Christian; it was redrawn in 1513 from pre-Christian maps found in the sacked library of Alexandria. It is called the Piri Re'is Map after the Turkish admiral who "found" it (*He* did not chart it). *It has its meridian in Egypt*, in the area later called Alexandria by the Greeks and Cairo by the Arabs. It definitely precedes them. Their maps do not show these things. The mid-Atlantic islands are shown with remarkable accuracy. *The Cape Verde, Madeira Islands and the Azores are shown in perfect longitude.* The Canary Islands are only off by one degree longitude. *The Andes are shown on this map. They were not seen by Europeans until 1527*, when Pizarro claimed to have "discovered" them. *The Atrato river in Columbia is shown for a distance of 300 miles from the sea. The Amazon river is also shown, the actual course of the river. In contrast, sixteenth-century European maps show no resemblance to its real course.* Even more remarkable is the near accuracy of the longitudinal and latitudinal coordinates between the African and American coasts (Covey, *Journal of African Civilizations*, vol. 8, no. 2, 1986:118– 135).[2] *No European map came even close to this until the eighteenth century. One hundred and fifty years after the death of Columbus, European encyclopedias declared that longitude had not been discovered and was probably undiscoverable.*

Below is what De Montellano et al. has to say about the Piri Re'is map. Dr. Finch, as well as Dr. Joan Covey, who first alerted me to this, have done a close study of the map and its origins. They systematically expose the deliberate and mendacious distortions of De Montellano et al.

Let me first quote my critics on the map. Please pay close attention to the distortions, both of the earlier commentators as well as those of

The Piri Re'is Map

my present critics. It is important to be on guard now, for we are facing not only prejudice and a compulsive desire to distort but an appallingly poor grasp of the critical facts.

"The map was pieced together," says De Montellano et al, "subsequent to the early Portuguese and Spanish voyages of discovery, and explicitly states on a marginal note that it includes a map of the "Western parts" obtained from Columbus (Bagrow [1951] 1985: 107–8; Soucek 1992:268) Thus, it is not surprising that "the Cape Verde, Madeira Islands and the Azores are shown in perfect longitude" (Van Sertima 1995:91) or that the map includes portions of the New World.

"Although based entirely on Hapgood, Van Sertima conveniently omits Hapgood's main conclusion, which provides no support for his thesis. If Hapgood is correct, the ancient Egyptians and Nubians were influenced by a superior civilization that emerged earlier in central Mexico, an idea that would be anathema to Van Sertima and his Afrocentric supporters with their agenda for promoting the anteriority and primacy of Nile Valley civilizations. If Hapgood is wrong, the Piri Re'is map becomes an ordinary portolan map reflecting current knowledge which proves nothing about the alleged transatlantic voyages by Egypto-Nubians and sub-Saharan Africans in the pre-Columbian period."

Now examine Dr. Finch's reply (dated 10 September 1997) to see the extent to which my trio of critics will go to distort history in order to promote their agenda.

In response to the paragraph cited by Montellano on the relevance of the Piri Re'is map, I will itemize the counterpoints below:

1. Montellano fails to mention that Piri Re'is states that *20* source maps were used to compile this map—the most accurate seen by the Western world until the nineteenth century—and only *one* came from Columbus. The other 19 source maps were dated to the time of Alexander. What is irrefutably certain is that no European navigator, certainly not Columbus, knew how to accurately determine longitude prior to 1744 when the chronometer was invented and came into widespread use by seamen. Whatever information was supplied by Columbus's material, it would never have allowed the accurate fixing of longitude evident everywhere on the Piri Re'is Map. Thus the determination of the "perfect longitudes" of Cape Verde, Madeira, and the Azores would have owed nothing to Columbus. However, we do know, on the basis of the pyramid studies by the most eminent astronomers of the 19th century, specifically Richard Proctor, that accurate longitude was obtainable by

Nile Valley priest-surveyors from their undoubted ability to determine the heavenly meridian(s).

2. Hapgood does indeed postulate the existence of a "prehistoric" world civilization, one that may go back 10,000 years or more. He is not alone in this surmise and a small but growing chorus of avant-garde antiquarians are asserting the same thing. He furthermore postulates, based on analyses done in past decades of the volcanic accumulation around one of the pyramids outside Mexico City, that some of these pyramids may be 7,000 years old and therefore may be a "relic" or outpost of an advanced world civilization that (by implication) possessed other centers elsewhere. *Nowhere does he infer that this world civilization arose in Mexico to spread over the rest of the world. Montellano is mendaciously distorting what Hapgood is actually claiming.* Looking at recent studies of the Egyptian Sphinx by geologists, we find that it is postulated that this monument and an advanced civilization to go with it is also 7-10,000 years old or older. Thus the presence of a very early ancient world civilization pre-existing what is customarily thought of as dynastic Egypt, lends nothing to Montellano's case because such an ancient world civilization *would have included Egypt itself!*

3. *Montellano also fails to mention that the center of the Map is 100 west of Aswan on the same meridian of Alexandria. To Hapgood, this means that the mapmaker was working in Egypt probably around 300 B.C., 30 years after Alexander founded his imperial capital, Alexandria, not in Greece but in Egypt!* Hapgood has also concluded that the source maps from which the ancient compilers were working that led to the Piri Re'is Map were actually *more accurate than the Piri Re'is Map itself!* Thus the Piri Re'is Map, as advanced as it is, actually represented a decline from older map-making standards! Working in Alexandria, the ancient cartographer(s) of the Piri Re'is Map had at their disposal much more precise world maps that could only have been drafted in Egypt itself. Where else could they have come from, particularly since the Great Pyramid represented the world's Prime Meridian of the time? Even the famous portolanos referred to owe nothing to European cartography; they derive from a map-making science preserved in the eastern and southern civilizations. Thus none of the portolanos represented "current" European knowledge during Medieval times. We must also remember the Ottoman Empire (to which Piri Re'is belonged) and its Arab predecessors, had controlled Egypt. Clearly, Islamic learning had emerged from surviving Greek and Egyptian writings. But the main point to remember is that the original Piri Re'is Map compilers lived and worked in Egypt 1800 years before Piri Re'is.

4. Peoples, goods, ideas, and techniques were flowing over the world by land and sea for thousands of years before Columbus. The "Age of Discovery," launched from the Iberian peninsula was merely the latest age of "Rediscovery." Africans crossed the Atlantic, the Indian Ocean, and the South China Seas. South Pacific Islanders, Chinese, and maybe

Japanese crossed the Pacific westward to make New World landfalls. Nor is there reason to doubt that Pre-Columbian Indian seafarers made trans-oceanic voyages The oceans were never a barrier between peoples and continents. They were a connecting link." (Dr. Charles Finch, 1997)

I had presented evidence in my earlier work of the influence of some Egyptian mummification practices on Peruvian mummification. Before I come to that question, it is necessary for me to expose another falsehood circulated by my critics who claim that mummification in South America preceded that of the Egyptian. They claim that the oldest mummies in the world are associated with the Chinchorro culture of Chile (Arriazza, 1995). That again is a bogus claim. The oldest mummy so far found is an infant mummy buried in Nubia (see photo). The Chinchorro mummy is dated 5,860 B.C. plus or minus 180 (Allison, 1985) but the infant mummy of Uan Muhuggiag is dated 7,438 B.C. plus or minus 220 (Professor E. Tongiori of the University of Pisa Carbon 14 assays). Reference to this Nubian mummy may be found in *Mummies, Diseases, and Ancient Cultures*, edited by Aidan and Eve Cockburn[3] (Cambridge CB2 1RP: Cambridge University Press 1980). The mummy was so named because it was unearthed beneath the Uan Muhuggiag natural rock shelter located in the Tagzelt Valley. Professor Mori's earlier carbon dating of this mummy was 3,500 B.C. but the University of Pisa carbon assays extended the age of the mummy by taking other factors into account. Tongiori's bracketed chronologies were deduced from more than one sampling venue. Since we are discussing ancient Egypto-Nubia and the spread of its civilization and it is particularly noted for its mummification, even to a schoolchild, how can a trio of apparently trained anthropologists make such a wild statement without first checking out the primacy of mummification practices in the Nile Valley?

There are several ways to mummify a body but Professor L. Ruetter has noted not only the same manner of evisceration through the anus and the same manner of swaddling the corpse in ritual bandages but, after a thorough analysis of embalming mixtures in Peru, that "the antiseptic substances used in embalming are identical with those used in ancient Egypt . . . balsam, menthol, salt, tannin, alkaloids, saponins and resins". The ingredients were available in Peru as they were in Egypt but the formula is complex and elusive.[4] (Ruetter, *Bulletin et Memoires Société d'Anthropologie*, 1915, p. 288) I will point to three unique and complex features which are common to ancient Egypt and Peru. A complex

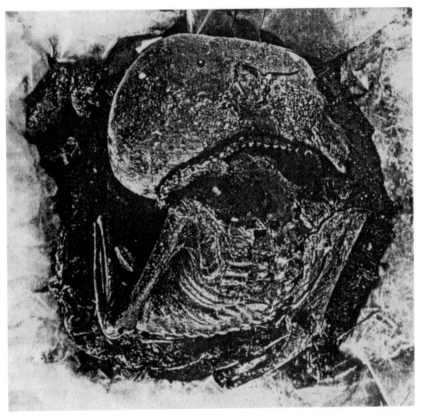

The infant mummy of Uan Muhuggiag (courtesy of F. Mori)

surgical procedure (trepannation) fitted megalithic masonry and two types of looms. These three are beyond dispute. Trepanning or trepannation was performed on the skulls of Egypto-Nubian soldiers, among others, to relieve pressure caused by blows on the skull. Hippocrates recommended it in an essay "On Injuries of the Head" in which he details the Egyptian procedure. We find the same complex and unique procedure performed by doctors in Peru. They removed plaques of bone from the skull and in many cases the operation was remarkably successful. Skulls examined in Peru, as in ancient Egypt, indicate absence of signs of infection and a new growth of normal bone in and about the wound. An examination of skulls in both Egypt and Peru upon which this operation was performed show square and circular holes in the skull. The skullbone was penetrated by scraping, cutting, or drilling the bone.[5] (William T. Corlett, *Medicine Man of the American Indian*, Springfield, Illinois, 1935, C.C. Thomas, pp. 38, 39)

Another shared feature calling for serious examination is "fitted megalithic masonry" The finest example of this is found at Saccsahuaman and Cuzco in Peru and, across the Pacific from Peru, on Easter Island. The technique calls for considerable skill, since the massive stone blocks fitted together are not of any regular shape or size (not cut in conventional squares) but display the complex regularity of patterns or designs in a jigsaw puzzle. No cement is used in the building of these massive blocks "so wonderfully exact is the masonry work, of which they are composed." Both ancient Egyptians and later the Peruvians quarried stone by "driving wooden wedges into natural faults in the stone, which cracked when the wedges filled with water."

Fitted megalithic masonry is unique to an area of the Old World (Egypto-Nubia) where a certain complex of cultural traits has been found. While the method of quarrying stone might have been coincidental, this method of building walls and fortifications was not. This technique only occurs where there is evidence of an Egyptian presence.

Other features that may be advanced as influences are the horizontal loom and the vertical-frame loom. Although native Americans in Peru were weaving cloth as early as 2,500 B.C. they were not using the loom. Dr. Junius Bird discovered cotton fabrics at Huaca Prieta in Peru carbon-dated 2,500 B.C. but 78 percent of the three thousand pieces of cotton were twined and the rest netted—two of the simplest methods of producing fabrics without a loom.[6] When a loom of the horizontal type appeared in Peru it was found to be "identical with a horizontal loom depicted in an Egyptian tomb" (Irwin, p.298) When the vertical loom appeared in Peru it was "identical with those found in a tomb at Thebes",[7] a sacred capital of the Egypto-Nubians. Both the New World and Old World looms had the same eleven working parts.[8] To be even more specific, it has been shown that "the vertical frame-loom with two warp beams used by the Incas was the same as that used in Egypt in the New Kingdom." (18th to 20th dynasty circa 1400–1100 B.C.).[9] It is important to note here that the earliest evidence of South American cocaine is found in the belly of Ramses II, which is even earlier than 1200 B.C. The second of the two types of Peruvian looms, the horizontal loom staked out on the ground, as used in the Titicaca basin, was also the same as that of ancient Egypt.[10] Spindle whorls, also used in weaving, were so identical in Egypt, the Mexican capital of Tula, and in Peru, that "laid side by side, even an expert can scarcely tell them apart.[11]

African in pre-Columbian Peru

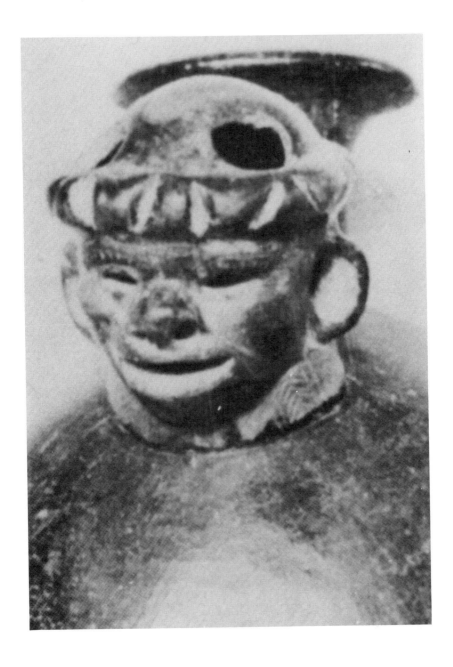

African in pre-Columbian Peru

African in pre-Columbian Peru

Descendants of black governors of Ecuador. Zambo chieftains from Esmereldas (in present-day Ecuador) who visited Quito in 1599. They are shown here in Spanish dress and Indian ornaments but were descendants of a group of 17 shipwrecked Africans who gained political control of an entire province of Ecuador in short order. (Cabello de Balboa, Obras, 1945, p. 133)

Plants and Transplants

I move now to the question of plants and transplants. Here again my critics have had a field day, misrepresenting my position on cotton and the African bottle-gourd and ignoring conveniently the evidence for the pre-Columbian marriage of an *African* and *South American* jackbean. Red seeds from Africa (*canavalia virosa*) intermarried with white seeds in South America (*canavalia plagiosperma*) to produce by repeated backcrossing in the Andean lowlands, a pre-Columbian African-American jackbean of brown seeds (*canavalia piperi*)[12] (*Meso-american Studies*, no. 6, p. 22). With regard to the cotton evidence, which considerations of space would not allow me to repeat here, I quote my opponent in the Smithsonian debate, Dr. David Kelley, about my examination of this matter. "Van Sertima's summary is a fair one, emphasizing that trans-Atlantic diffusion is more reasonable than trans-Pacific diffusion in this case, a view supported not only by the geography but by the fact that Near Eastern cotton is the wrong kind, and that it and Indian cotton are too late for the American cottons"[13] (Kelley, 1995, pp. 103–122). My critics say that I claim the cotton was brought in during the Egypto-Nubian voyages. I *never said so*. They also claim that I said man came in with the bottle gourd when I was at pains to point out that it was *the one plant that could drift to America without man without loss of seed viability*.

"Bottle gourds", I quote[14] (*They Came*, p. 204) got caught in the pull of currents from the African coast and drifted to America across the Atlantic. Thomas Whitaker and G.F. Carter showed that gourds are capable of floating in seawater for 7 months without loss of seed viability." Yet my critics declare: "There is no need to posit human transport for this plant to the New World. Additionally, it makes little sense for persons accidentally making a sea voyage to load up the boat with these bulky, nearly inedible fruits."[15] Now what is this but deliberate misrepresentation? They even claim that "the presence of the gourd in the New World predates any domestication in West Africa". Again, that is not true. The species originated in tropical Africa and, as botanists I.H. Burkhill and Oaks Ames, have shown, was originally domesticated there.[16] (*Mesoamerican Studies*, no.6). Let me say again in closing: What I have sought to prove is not that Africans "discovered" America but that they made contact with this continent long before Columbus. The whole notion of any people (European, African, or American) "discovering" a civilization is absurd. Such notions should be abandoned once and for all. They presume some innate superiority in the "discoverer" and something inferior or barbaric in the people "discovered." What I have sought to prove is not that Africans "discovered" America but that they made contact on several occasions before Saint Christopher, at least two of which were culturally significant for Americans.

Twenty-one years have passed since *They Came Before Columbus* was published. I have studiously avoided repeating my own work. The Random House book is a work to be read by all, not only deeply steeped in the history of an earlier time, an earlier Africa, an earlier America, as this work is, but also an earlier style, charged with the drama of ancient times, events and places, in spite of its grounding in the facts of history. This, my latest essay on the subject, presents a number of new facts that were not known twenty-one years ago but it is forged out of a burning desire to restate and update the case in the clearest possible manner. It is also forged and fueled out of an anger at the dishonesty of my critics and an overwhelming desire to set the record straight. These two books do not cancel out each other. It is as if they were written by brother-spirits, not by the same person.

I look back on my earlier work, as if reading it for the first time. I look over what I have done during the past year and I know I have learnt a great deal during the last two decades that establish my work on an even firmer base since I have edited a dozen anthologies on African civilizations in the interim. But these works in no way compete with each other nor is the latest to be seen as a sequel to the earlier. I am revisiting a house I never really left, a house of many floors, many rooms, some of which I had never lived in as fully during my first occupancy of the site.

Notes

1. Van Sertima to Cheikh Anta Diop and Diop's reply appears in the 1979 issue of *Journal of African Civilizations* (vol. 1, no. 2).
2. Joan Covey, *Journal of African Civilizations*, vol. 8, no. 2, 1986: p. 118–135.
3. *Mummies, Diseases and Ancient Cultures* (eds. Aidan and Eve Cockburn) Cambridge CB2 RP: Cambridge University Press, 1980 (see M.J. Carter's essay in J.A.C., vol. 12, 1994.
4. Ruetter, *Bulletin et Memoires Société d'Anthropologie*, 1915, p. 288
5. William T. Corlett, *Medicine Man of the American Indian*, Springfield, Illinois, 1935, C.C. Thomas, pp. 38, 39.
6. Constance Irwin, *Fair Gods and Stone Faces*, St. Martin's Press, 1963 p. 298.
7. Irwin, Idem.
8. Kenneth Mc Gowan, *Early Man in The New World*, New York, MacMillan.
9. Heyerdahl in Ashe, *The Quest for America*, p. 134
10. Ibid. Idem.
11. Irwin, op. cit. pp. 297, 298.
12. Karl Schwerin, "Winds across the Atlantic" (*Mesoamerican Studies*, no. 6, p. 22)
13. David Kelley, *Race, Discourse and the Origin of the Americas* (eds. Vera Hyatt and Rex Nettleford (Smithsonian Institution Press (Washington and London, 1995)
14. Ivan Van Sertima, *They Came Before Columbus* (Random House, 1976)
15. De Montellano et al., *Current Anthropology* (June 1997)
16. Schwerin, *Mesoamerican Studies*, no. 6
17. Harold Lawrence, "African Explorers in the New World," *Crisis*, June-July 1962, Heritage Program Reprint, p. 10
18. J.V. Luce in Geoffrey Ashe (ed), *The Quest for America*, New York, Praeger Publishers, 1971, pp. 90, 91.

4

Reply to My Critics

An attack on my thesis that Africans made contact with America before Columbus in two major pre-Christian periods (circa 1200 B.C. and circa 800 B.C.) in addition to the Mandingo contact period (A.D. 1310/1311) has been circulated in advance to hundreds of subscribers to a journal, Current Anthropology. Copies of this attack by Bernard de Montellano, Warren Barbour and Gabriel Haslip-Viera were also sent out to African-American scholars, some of whom were cited in the attack, dishonestly titled "Van Sertima's Afrocentricity and the Olmecs". The title's emphasis is meant to suggest that all revisions of African history by so called "blacks" belong to a common school, radiate from a common brain, and are cast in the same "racialist" hue and mode. This circular, which precedes my new book *Early America Revisited* (scheduled to appear in April, 1998) seeks to highlight the brazen and malicious lies, slanders and misrepresentations that characterize this attack. Let it be noted that I was invited to respond to this attack but was forced to withdraw. The editor, after verbally agreeing that I could reprint my commentary, after the issue of the Journal appeared, did a dramatic about-turn when pressed to sign a written agreement to back up his word. He wrote that I could only reprint my "commentary" (15 pages) if I also reprinted the attack on me (50 pages) since "they form a unit." To feel the full absurdity of this, just imagine the Jewish Defense League being forced to republish an extended Nazi-type attack on their positions in order to republish a brief response to such a slanderous attack.

LIE ONE: "Van Sertima's expedition allegedly sailed or drifted westward to the Gulf of Mexico where it came in contact with inferior

Olmecs. These individuals created Olmec civilization". —De Montellano, Barbour and Haslip-Viera.

THE TRUTH: As far back as 1976, I made my position on this matter very clear. I never said that Africans created or founded American civilization. I said they made contact and all significant contact between two peoples lead to influences. "I think it is necessary to make it clear—since partisan and ethnocentric scholarship seems to be the order of the day—that the emergence of the Negroid face. which the archeological and cultural data overwhelmingly confirm, in no way presupposes the lack of a native originality, the absence of other influences or the automatic eclipse of other faces"—p. 147 of *They Came Before Columbus*. See also *Journal of African Civilizations*, vol. 8, no. 2, 1986 "I cannot subscribe to the notion that civilization suddenly dropped onto the American earth from the Egyptian heaven."

LIE TWO: None of the early Egyptians and Nubians looked like Negroes. "They have long, narrow noses . . . "Short, flat noses are confined to the West African ancestors of African-Americans" Again, "there is no evidence that ancient Nubians ever braided their hair. This style comes from colonial and modern Ethiopia.

THE TRUTH: Narrow noses have been found among millions of pure-blooded Africans. We can see this among the Elongated and Nilotic types. My critics know nothing about the variants of Africa, ancient or modern. All the six main variants of the African have been found in Egyptian and Nubian graves. For examples of ancient braided Nubian hair, see Frank Snowden's "Before Color Prejudice". As for Egypto-Nubians only having narrow noses, see Egyptian pharaohs in vol. 10 and 12 of the JAC and major Nubian pharaohs in Peggy Bertram's essay (JAC vol. 12); Ushanaru, plate 8, p 173; Taharka as the god Amun from Kawa Temples, plate 9, p. 173; Shabaka, plate 12, p. 176. Tanwetamani, plate 16, p. 180. To say that these are narrow noses is to exhibit a colossal ignorance of African types in ancient Egypt and Nubia. The agenda behind this is to bolster their case that they could not have been models for any of the Olmec stone heads.

LIE THREE: Modern Egyptians look exactly as they did thousands of years ago. The composition of the Egyptian has not changed over the last 5000 years. Invasions by the Assyrians, Persians, Greeks, Arabs and Romans left them looking the same today as in the dawn of history.

THE TRUTH: This is a hasty misreading of the work of scholars like A.C. Berry, RJ. Berry and Ucko who point out that there is a remarkable degree of homogeneity in this area for 5000 years. What a superficial reading of this fails to note is that the period ends with the close of the native dynasties *before* the invasions of the Assyrian, Persian, Greek, Roman, and Arab foreigners.

LIE FOUR: Faced with the startlingly Negroid features of some of the Olmec stone heads, my critics try four ways out (a) They are spitting images of the natives (b) They appear dark because some of them were carved out of dark volcanic stone (c) some were made of white basalt which turned dark over time (d) ancient Egyptians and Nubians were remote in physiognomy from sub-Saharan Negroes and none of them could have been models for any of the Negro-looking heads. Having said all that, they then claim that races are not linked to specific physiognomic traits.

THE TRUTH: No need to shoot them down on this. They turned the gun on themselves.

LIE FIVE: Nothing African has been found in any archeological excavation in the New World.

THE TRUTH: In the drier centers of the Olmec world—at Tlatilco, Cerro de las Mesas and Monte Alban—Polish craniologist, Andrez Wiercinski, found indisputable evidence of an African presence. The many traits analyzed in these Olmec sites indicated individuals with Negroid traits predominating but with an admixture of other racial traits. This is what I have said. The work of A. Vargas Guadarrama is an important reinforcement of Wiercinski's study. He found that the skulls he had examined at Tlatilco, which Wiercinski had classified as Negroid, were radically different from other skulls on the site, bearing indisputable similarities to skulls in West Africa and Egypt.

LIE SIX: Van Sertima presents no evidence that a New World cotton (*gossypium hirsutum var. punctatum*) transferred from Guinea to the Cape Verde in 1462 by the Portuguese and there is no hard proof that West Africans made a round trip to America before Columbus.

THE TRUTH: I cited evidence in twelve categories to establish Mandingo voyages to the New World circa A.D. 1310/1311. This included eyewitness reports from nearly a dozen Europeans, even Columbus himself, metallurgical, linguistic, botanical, navigational, oceanographic, skeletal, epigraphic, cartographic. oral, documented and iconographic evidence. With regard to New World cotton in Africa before 1462, Stephens spoke in two tongues to pacify isolationist colleagues. (See his statement in *Early America Revisited*)

LIE SEVEN: My critics claim that I said the bottle gourd came in with Old World voyagers.

THE TRUTH: I was at pains to point out that this is *one plant that could drift to America without the loss of seed viability*. "Bottle gourds got caught in the pull of currents from the African coast and drifted to America across the Atlantic. Thomas Whitaker and G.F. Carter showed that these gourds are capable of floating in seawater for 7 months without loss of seed viability"—They Came Before Columbus, 204. They indulge in an even more vicious dishonesty with regard to cotton, claiming that I said "Old World cottons came into America with a fleet of Nubians circa 700 B.C." I never linked cotton transfer to Nubian contact.

LIE EIGHT: My critics admit "we cannot unequivocally date the heads but they single out one which they say Ann Cyphers confidently dated about 1011 B.C. Note the date! This is 200 years *after* the Egyptian contact period c. 1200 B.C. Yet they claim that the dating of this one head proves "Negro-looking heads" were being carved, mutilated, and buried prior to 1200 B.C.

THE TRUTH: The stone heads could not have been buried before they were carved.

LIE NINE: Egyptians stopped building pyramids "thousands of years" before 1200 B.C. No relation whatever exists between Old World/New World pyramids.

THE TRUTH: Enormous obelisks, calling for the same complex engineering skills of the pyramid age were built at Karnak as late as 1295 B.C. A pyramid was also built at Dashur circa 1700 B.C. Bart Jordan, the mathematical child prodigy, to whom Einstein granted special audience, established startling coincidences between Old World and New World pyramids. He agrees with me that "The overwhelming incidence of coincidence argues overwhelmingly against a mere coincidence." (see his two contributions to *Early America Revisited*)

LIE TEN: My critics claim that I have trampled upon the self-respect and self-esteem of native Americans and they have come forward to champion their cause.

THE TRUTH: My people (for I am part Macusi and part African) would be horrified to have, as champion of our cause, De Montellano, Barbour, and Haslip-Viera, who disgrace us with the charge that "native Americans would have sacrificed and eaten the Africans if they came."

LIE ELEVEN: The oldest mummies in the world are associated with the Chinchorro culture of Chile (Arriazza 1995)

THE TRUTH: The oldest mummy so far found is an infant mummy buried in Nubia. The Chinchorro mummy is dated 5,860 B.C. plus or minus 180 (Allison 1985) but the infant mummy of Uan Muhuggiag is dated 7,438 B.C. plus or minus 220 (Professor E. Tongiori of the University of Pisa Carbon 14 assays). Reference to the mummy is contained in *Mummies, Diseases and Ancient Cultures* edited by Aidan and Eve Cockburn. (Cambridge CB2 IRP, Cambridge University Press). The mummy was so named because it was unearthed beneath the Uan Muhuggiag rock shelter located in the Tagzelt Valley. Professor Mori's earlier carbon-dating of this mummy was 3,500 B.C. but the University of Pisa carbon assays extended the age of the mummy by taking other factors into account. Tongiori's bracketed chronologies were deduced from more than one sampling venue.

LIE TWELVE: The African cotton gossypium herbarium could not have been an ancestor of one of the American cottons. The only cotton that could have affected American wild cottons was the Pacific cotton gossypium tormentosum.

THE TRUTH: There is no cotton by the name of gossypium herbarium. Van Sertima spoke of the African cultivated cotton gossypium herbaceum. Both Dr. David Kelley, Van Sertima's opponent in the Smithsonian debate, as well Dr Karl Schwerin, who has done the definitive thesis on this subject: *Winds across the Atlantic (Mesoamerican Studies*, no. 6) agree with Van Sertima on this issue. Our trio of critics exhibit both ignorance as well as a pretense at knowledge on a matter they have never investigated. There is no cotton by the name of gossypium herbarium. A herbarium is a collection of plants systematically arranged or a room or building in which such a collection of plants is kept. It is not a plant at all. Dr Schwerin was as appalled as I was by the pretension of my critics to be plant experts and yet did not even know the basics of plant storage and cultivation. Since there are three of them playing this "*Slander Van*" game, couldn't just one of them have looked up a primer on botany or asked a freshman in a botany class, so as not to expose their already transparent disguise as experts?

LIE THIRTEEN: There are no Nubian pyramids of the eighth and seventh century B.C. that are stepped pyramids. A diagram of a "typical" Nubian pyramid that appears in Lumpkin (JAC, 1992, p. 146) appears to be stepped, but it also has a top that comes to a point. This suggests that the "alleged" steps had no functional purpose, which is the complete opposite of Mesoamerican practice.

THE TRUTH: The Egyptian Egyptologist, Ahmed Fakhry (1969, p. 140-141) in his description of the pyramids of El Kurru, wrote "Each had a superstructure built around a core of mud, and small, rough pieces of stone, covered with a smooth or *stepped* sandstone casing". Again, in describing the pyramids of Nuri, Fakhry wrote, "Some are stepped; others have smooth casings". Again, pyramid expert I. E. S. Edwards in *The Pyramids of Egypt*, 1979, p. 289, said that the steps, even though covered, were retained because of of their religious significance (see Beatrice Lumpkin's reply in this volume.)

LIE FOURTEEN: De Montellano et al claim that the Piri Re'is map of South America was pieced together subsequent to Columbus and was not a pre-Columbian map at all, that the "western parts" were obtained from Columbus and that, therefore, "it is not surprising that the Cape Verde, Madeira Islands and the Azores are shown in perfect longitude."

THE TRUTH: The Piri Re'is map was found in the sacked library of Alexandria. The center of the map is 100° west of Aswan on the same meridian of Alexandria in Egypt. Only one piece that was later added to this pre-Christian map comes from Columbus, only one. Neither Columbus nor anyone living between 1492 and 1744 (when the chronometer was invented) could plot longitude. Thus the determination of perfect longitudes of Cape Verde, Madeira, and the Azores owes nothing to Columbus (see Dr Finch's response to this lie in the South American section of *Early America Revisited*).

There are several pre-Christian elements in the Piri Re'is map that were unknown, except by the Egyptians, until as late as the 16th century. Joan Covey, who has also done an exhaustive study of this map, points to quite a number of these:

"The Andes are shown on this map. The Andes were not "discovered" until 1527 by Pizarro. The Atrato river (in present day Colombia) is shown for a distance of 300 miles from the sea. Its eastward bend at 5° north latitude is correct. Latitude was difficult to determine correctly in the era of Columbus. A long time after his four voyages, Haiti and Cuba were placed above rather than below the Tropic of Cancer. The Canary Islands in the Piri Re'is map is only off by 1° longitude. The Andes are also shown. They were not seen by Europeans until 1527, when Pizarro claimed to have "discovered" them. The Atrato river in Colombia is shown for a distance of 300 miles from the sea. The Amazon river is also shown, the actual course of the river. In contrast, sixteenth century European maps show no resemblance to its real course" (Joan Covey, J.A.C, vol. 8, no. 2)

Interview for "Our Time" (Part One)

by David Greaves
New York, 1997

David Greaves: I've heard about you, heard about your work, but I had not read it. But reading it, I'm saying, "My God, I have to relearn everything." Throw out all the stuff I grew up with—"Columbus sailing the ocean blue in 1492," and start over from scratch. I find it sad and angering.

Jacqueline Van Sertima: What's wonderful to me is that you want to do it. There are a lot of people who don't want to do it. Whether it's true or not, they feel it's safer to stay put in whatever they are.

Ivan Van Sertima: It was even harder for me because all my early training was that Africans were primitives. I really believed that. Then I decided, after four years in the Central Office of Information in England, to do a degree in African studies. I went to one of the best universities in the world for that but all the data available and most of the approaches in that time were racist, whether intentional or not. They concentrated on obscure face-to-face communities in little villages or in the jungle. At the end of the first year I tried to commit suicide.

DG: Really!

IVS: Yes. That was at the School of Oriental and African Studies. They've changed a lot since then, I'm sure. But what I learned there in my twenties frightened me because we colonials had already grown up with a total disrespect for ourselves. Almost everything I learnt in the university consolidated my self-hatred, self-contempt. We never thought Africans or people of African descent amounted to anything. But one thing had entered my life that was to save me. It was as if a lifebuoy had been thrown down into the darkness of my waters. I was deeply involved in literature. I wrote the first study of Caribbean writers. It was broadcast by the British as well as the Germans and the French. Then something happened that was to shift my focus, realign my sights forever. I fell upon the strange and haunting tale of The Palm Wine Drinkard by the African writer Tutuola and then upon a novel by a Nigerian, Chinua Achebe. I was stunned by the prose poetry of Tutuola and the attempt at the evocation of a century by Achebe in his book "Things Fall Apart." The axis of my world shifted. It was not that Achebe was a genius. Some of the authors from the Caribbean were more talented (Wilson Harris, for example, whom I recommended for the Nobel Prize in Literature, when I was invited by the Nobel Committee of the Swedish Academy to nominate candidates for the Nobel Prize in Literature [1976–1980]). What struck me was that I had never dreamt, after our fragmentation, after our being scattered like leaves in the wind, we could still capture the essence of a lost time, a shattered world, a vanished century. I began to realize I knew nothing about Africa. What had been fed me were crumbs from the master's table. I knew next to nothing about my true heritage and, what was worse, I did not know that it could even be recovered. Then I began to read everything the Africans had written in the English and French-dominated worlds. Then I went to one of my superior officers in the Central Office of Information. "Now that I've finished Caribbean writers," I said, "I'd like to do a study of African writers." His face turned red with amazement and dismay. "African writers? Come now, Van Sertima. You did so well with the Caribbean writers. But don't go jumping overboard. I appreciate your feelings. Africans did some remarkable things. But surely not in literature. They never even had a script."

That's not true. sir. But even if it were true of some of them, neither did the English nor the Spanish nor the French, nor the Dutch, nor the Germans have scripts. You are all using Roman script. I mean no disrespect, sir, but you were all ancient illiterates. The Romans conquered you and gave you a script.

DG: He was not in love with you for that.

IVS: But you see they respected me for all the broadcasts I had done, not just in that field, so he said graciously. "You have a point there. But I'm sorry. You can't do that." So I said: I think my time is up here, sir. I'm resigning. "O no. no. no." He looked genuinely concerned. "You've been doing such good work here. We're so proud of you."

DG: We've been so proud of you until now.

IVS: Yes sir, I said, I appreciate that. But I really want to do a series on African Writers. If I can't do that, I think I would rather resign. "No. No." he said "You leave here and you go into the wilderness. Don't do it just to prove a point. I'll see to it that they promote you". Promote me to what? I asked. "Well," he said, "we could make you head of something. What about head of the post room?"

JVS: That's the mail room.

IVS: It's a good job, sir, I said, but that's not exactly my dream in life, "Okay, old boy, what do you want to do?" I want to go to a university. "We could try and arrange that," he said seriously. That is how I got into the School of Oriental and African Studies. I was so excited at first. The very first week I arrived I was invited to a party at the house of Count von Heimendorf. A lot of celebrated authorities on Africa were there. But almost all the anthropological studies in Africa then were studies of primitives or "simple peoples", as they called them. They would go out into the bush or some little village and build a kinship chart. A sort of map of relationships. Who is one's grandmother, grandfather, mother, father, sister, brother, daughter, son. Then they would begin to learn about all their little rituals. It was like studying the family network and behavior of strange little monkeys. Nothing about their complexities, mind you, their sciences. They were not supposed to have science. I was the first person to edit a book on early African sciences. They drummed this primitive stuff into me day after day. It drove me to the depths of despair. At the end of the first year I took poison. I went into a coma for about three days. The chief doctor said afterwards that I must have drank enough poison to kill three Englishmen. Probably because I had grown up in a forest village I had resistance to certain poisons that would have killed an Englishman. I don't know. All I know is that I survived. But I was never the same again.

DG: What had changed for you?

IVS: I couldn't think about Africans in the same way. I couldn't think about the British in the same way.

Bernice Green: You said you started thinking of Africans and the British in a different way. Could you elaborate?

IVS: Well, at that time, I had lived for 29 years as a British colonial. There was one period of my life when my people—the people of Guyana—had a great hope for a new world. The British controlled everything at first but in 1953 we were given the vote and thus for the first time a chance to choose our leaders, a chance at independence. The East Indians and the Africans came together as one for the very first time. And for the first time we built such an unbeatable coalition of the races that we were swept to power. That power lasted for 133 days. There was a fear that we would become another Cuba. The British grew alarmed and suspended our Constitution. Charges were brought against the ruling party and some of its leaders were thrown into prison. The object was to make sure that the spirit of resistance would be broken forever, that we would never see ourselves again as one united people. All sorts of divisive rumors were fed into the system. We ended up fighting among ourselves, some of us actually beginning to see our former masters as our only salvation. Some of us were murdered at the hands of our former comrades. Some of us were thrown into prison. All our hopes died. The terrible thought returned. We must be as they have taught us—an inferior people. It was a terrible disillusionment. Perhaps, I thought, we would have to live with those images. First, jungle bunnies, then slaves, then colonial mimic-men. Extensions of other people, other peoples.

DO: What brought you to America?

IVS: It was a curious destiny that brought me here. I arrived in fact by accident. My prime minister, Forbes Burnham, had invited me back to

Guyana because it was celebrating its independence and I was called there to read poetry. At that time I was known for my poetry and my literary essays. As I was preparing to return to England, Jan Carew, who is one of our famous authors and who at that time was a professor at Princeton, invited me to come to America and visit him on my way back to Britain. I had no proper job, very little money. But he pointed out that my plane landed at Kennedy Airport on its way to London and I could drop off in New York, take a taxi to Port Authority, a bus to Princeton, and join a plane to London later. That was the beginning of a whole new life for me. I came to Princeton on a Saturday evening. When I awoke on Sunday morning Carew was asleep. So I came downstairs and began to browse through his library. Then the miracle began to unfold.

I saw three green books—*Africa and the Discovery of America* by Leo Wiener. He was a German-American professor. I opened the first book of the trilogy and started reading. I was extremely skeptical. Africans in America before Columbus? This man must be crazy. The books were thick but I scanned them rapidly. What startled me at first was to find that Columbus was the chief witness on the stand. What a shock it was to me, in spite of all that I had recoiled at in the British school of anthropology, in spite of the fact that I had steeped myself in the rich new literature of the Caribbean and Africa. I had been well trained by my imperial masters. I could not easily accept this. I would have to check out every word, every claim. I came back to America a few months later. I got a job at Rutgers teaching "Swahili Literature in Translation" and "Oral Tradition in Language and Literature". I found one or two weak elements in the Wiener thesis and actually started out doing a critique of it. I ended up by saying, "If anyone could show me the image of one African in America before Columbus, I would begin to believe". That was the problem with Wiener. No images of the African. He knew nothing of the terracotta. As for the stone-heads (some of which had distinctly African features) they had not yet been discovered. No one knew then of the Africoid skeletons that could back up the evidence in paintings and sculpture. The problem with Wiener was that he was first and foremost a linguist. A few surviving words from Africa would not be enough. He had very few pictures and not a single one of them was of an African sculpted in the period he concentrated upon. A thesis as revolutionary as this could not stand alone on the fragile pillars of philology.

I sent my critical appraisal of the thesis to a magazine editor at Random House. They were preparing the second issue of a magazine called *Amistad*. I ended my critique of Wiener with the words "If anyone could show me the unmistakable image of an African in America in a pre-Columbus period, I would take another hard look at this matter."

The editor of *Amistad* called me a week later. "Van Sertima, something strange has happened on my desk. I had just finished reading your critique of Leo Wiener. When I turned the last page, expressing your doubts, I came upon six photographs. John Williams, the novelist, has just come back from Mexico. There he met a strange German—Baron Alexander Von Wuthenau. He was once secretary to the German Embassy in Washington, D.C. He has the images you were looking for. Von Wuthenau has spent quarter of a century checking these things out. I said to myself. "O my God, how can I throw a question out in space and the answer comes back before the same eyes, in the same space, the answer and the question actually kissing each other?" So I flew straight to Mexico that weekend to see this man. He was in his late seventies or early eighties but we were both so excited by our common quest that we sat on the steps of his chateau and talked and talked almost right through the long summer night.

DBJ: Did you begin to believe in the thesis after that meeting?

IVS: I began to realize that the proof lay in many disciplines. That Wiener was isolated in linguistics, Von Wuthenau in the sculptural evidence. I would have to enter a dozen rooms, or, to put it another way, look out on the past through a dozen windows. Sometimes in my imaging of the past I felt as if something akin to an explosion had occurred and one had to put the pieces back together to find out what happened. The method they use in aeroplane crashes would be the method one would have to use in the flight and fall of cultures. So I went searching for the pieces in every possible discipline—in oral and written sources, in sculptures, in paintings, in the crossing of plants from one continent to another, in the duplication of complex ritual phenomena that had clear antecedence in one place and had never turned up before in the other, in extraordinary linguistic linkages, in skeletal remains, in references found in ancient and medieval documents. I turned up twelve categories of evidence in the case of the presence of Mandingo types among the native Americans in the 14th century Caribbean and Mexico. Von Wuthenau's study of the terracotta that had emerged from excavations and museums made me see the faces of Africans who had wandered into this territory before Columbus.

DG: And once you see the stone heads which I saw in your book *African Presence in Early America* you cannot argue with the evidence.

IVS: But my major critics claim that I "doctored the photographs" to make these people look like Africans.

DG: That's unbelievable.

IVS: Anyway, I don't want to talk about the stone heads at this point because I want to concentrate in the first half of our interview on the Mandingo journeys, A.D. 1310 and 1311. We will deal with the early pre-Christian contact period (1200 B.C.) at a later date. It involves Africans of another time from another place and we shall call upon another body of evidence.

BG: Your book *They Came Before Columbus* impacted on many people. We're here because we want to bring you and it into the year 2000. We think that there is a movement to have it go away and die.

IVS: The critics will die long before that book. I rewrote it three times. Every time I finished I found something new. I am still discovering things. I am now working on a new book "Early America Revisited". This will be a reply to my critics and I will restate and update the case because I have come upon a whole body of even harder evidence that makes a mockery of the silly and vicious criticisms that are being showered upon me now. I was fascinated by the villain of the piece—Christopher Columbus himself. I found a description of him at table with the king of Portugal, Don Juan. They had a heated discussion. And it is clear that the Portuguese knew of land to the west even before Columbus had sailed. They learnt this from Africans and there are documents to prove it. These are not "invented scenarios" as my critics claim. I cite the sources which they so conveniently ignore. I recreate the face, even the expression on the face, of Don Juan. He had a sickness which gave him a drooping face. That's how I began. I was so astonished at times how one discovery would lead to another. There are machines that give off a buzz when they hone in to hidden objects . . . My brain became for a while almost like that. I would feel a curious sensation like a kind of buzz as I walked through the aisles of libraries. One would not normally open some of these books because the titles do not relate at all to the subject one is exploring but there is something there for you—a paragraph perhaps, sometimes just a footnote. What startled me most and I think I have said that before, was to find that Columbus was the chief witness.

He actually wrote in his Journal of the Second Voyage that when he was in Haiti, the native Americans came to them and told them that black-skinned people had come from the south and south-east trading in gold-tipped metal spears. Columbus may not have believed but he actually sent two of these spears back to Spain and they were inspected microscopically in Spain and found to be identical, not just similar, *identical* in their ratio of gold, silver, and copper alloys to spears being forged in Guinea They were composed of thirty-two parts—eighteen of gold, six of silver and eight of copper. And all the words for the spears had identical sounds that Africans were using on the other side of the Atlantic. Now how can you argue with that? And, as I probed further into the matter, I discovered that it was not just Christopher Columbus but a dozen Europeans who claimed they saw, or heard from other Europeans who saw, these Africans. My critics claim this is just an Afrocentric theory. Then Columbus and his son and all the explorers who came, *who saw*, who conquered, were all Afrocentrics, if one follows the logic of this silly argument.

Ferdinand Columbus, one of the four sons of Columbus, said "my father told me he saw Negroes north of Honduras." Then there is *Vasco Nuñez de Balboa* coming down the slopes of Quarequa, which is near Darien, which we now call Panama. We have it down to the day—25 September 1513. He sees two tall Black men among the native Americans. This is not the era of the African slave trade. The Spanish were utterly startled (so startled that four of them comment on it) and they asked the natives from whence did these Black men come. They did not know. All that they knew was that they lived in a large settlement near by and they were waging war with them and had captured these two. These Africans are described in detail. Exceedingly black, a foot-and-a-half taller than the average Native American, of military bearing. *Peter Martyr*, the first historian of the European contact period, said that these Blacks must have been shipwrecked long ago from Africa (he called it Ethiopia which was then a general word for Africa from the word *aethiops*, meaning burnt skin). You also have other commentators like *Lopez de Gomara* who wrote that "these blacks Balboa saw were identical with the blacks we have seen in Guinea". *Rodrigo de Colmenares* reported that one of the captains of Balboa saw blacks east of the Gulf of San Miguel". Then *Alphonse de Quatrefages*, author of "The Human Species" presents us with a map drawn by a French sea-captain, Kerhallet, showing independent black settlements in the area later called Brazil. Also, at the tip of Florida, and on the island of St. Vincent. This can account for the Charruas of Brazil, the Jamassi of Florida, and the Black Caribs of St. Vincent. They were all pre-Columbian Black settlements. *Captain Kerhallet* presents a map of these settlements and that is the area, that very area, that is the endpoint or terminus of currents flowing in across the Atlantic from Africa. The Africans appeared exactly where the ocean current from Africa takes you.

Few people are aware that there are natural sea-roads. I call them "marine conveyor belts". That is what they really are. Once you are caught in these currents and you do not have an engine (and no one had engines at that point in time) you have to come to America. The better your ship and knowledge of the ocean, the more likely you will come on purpose. The worse your ship and seamanship, the more likely you'll come by mistake. Look at this map.

DG: That's a very powerful map, that map of the currents. As soon as you see it, you say, "Yeah, that's right."

IVS: That was the problem with early pioneers like Wiener. He didn't do that. Most scholars do not do that. They think words are enough. But pictures speak much louder than words. That is often the definitive proof, the definitive evidence. My opponents cannot argue with that. So they accuse me of using forged artifacts and doctoring the photos.

In the next installment Van Sertima cites another half-dozen Europeans who sighted Blacks in America during the Mandingo contact period. He then goes on to present evidence for an even earlier contact with a major American civilization—that of the Olmec. He speaks also of what can be done to give a new vision to America's youth. He exposes the current attempt by his opponents to misrepresent his thesis. Also, their sinister campaign to get teachers and administrators to keep his many edited books on African civilization from entering the curriculum of the schools.

Interview for "Our Time" (Part Two)

by David Greaves
New York, 1997

In the first installment of our interview with Ivan Van Sertima, he cited seven Europeans who actually saw or heard of Africans when they first came to America. Among these witnesses to an African presence was Christopher Columbus himself, his son, Ferdinand Columbus, Vasco Nuñez de Balboa, Peter Martyr, Lopez de Gomara, Rodrigo de Colmenares and a French sea-captain, Kerhallet. These Africans were sighted among the native Americans at the very points at which the currents from Africa end in America, Van Sertima refers to these swiftly moving currents as "marine conveyor belts". In this second instalment he cites half a dozen more European witnesses to an African presence in America before Columbus and goes on to present evidence of an even earlier contact with a major American civilization—the Olmec.

IVS: In addition to the European explorers of the Columbus contact period I have so far cited, there is L'Abbé Brasseur de Bourbourg who comes down into Panama and studies Panama before the slave trade. He found there were two indigenous people—the red-skinned people(native Americans) known as the Tule, and a Black-skinned people, known as the Mandinga. These would be the Africans who came in during the 1310–1311 journeys from the West African empire of Mali, which empire, according to the Arabs, who had crossed it by caravan, was as large in that time as all the states of Western Europe put together. According to the oral tradition of Mali and two Arabic documents—*Masalik el-Absar fir Mamelik el Amsar* and *al-Qalquashandi*—two journeys across the western ocean were attempted during the reign of the Mandingo king, Abu Bakari II. He headed the second expedition to the Americas himself and did not return.

Then we have Alonzo Ponce who, when he lands in Campeche off Mexico, is told by the natives that black-skinned people had come in large boats before the Spanish. Ponce refers to them as Moors, which then was the Spanish term for "Blacks."

Then there is Riva Palacio who claimed they found Black-skinned people off Tegucigalpa on the Nicaraguan-Honduran border. There is also Ramon Pane, a priest. He speaks of the Black "guanini", meaning the black gold traders since the African word ghana, ghanin etc. was used for the gold-tipped spears in which the early Africans traded. Rodrigo de Colmenares, one of the captains of Balboa, also reported he saw blacks east of the Gulf of San Miguel. And so we have a dozen Europeans who reported they saw Blacks.

BG: What about graves and burial sites?

IVS: That is one of the most startling pieces of evidence. I went down to the Virgin Islands when I heard the story that they had found two Africans in a pre-Columbian grave at Hull Bay in St. Thomas. The Associated Press report, published in the *Washington Post*, said that they had been found in a pre-Columbian grave dated A.D. 1250. That means the strata or ground level in which they were found was so dated. This is called stratigraphical dating. They could not carbon date the bones themselves because something unexplainable had interfered with the carbon levels. However, they did say that these skeletons exhibited a dental ritual—filing of incisor teeth—peculiar to some Atlantic coast Africans. They also said that they found a pre-Columbian native ornament clamped around the forearm of one of the skeletons. After I reported this far and wide there was silence about these African bones for about twenty years. A few months ago, however, an anthropologist in the Virgin Islands, who thought that I had not investigated the matter in person and in detail, ran a story saying that the African skeletons had to be post-Colombian because they had dental disease, suggesting that Africans, being primitive, could not get dental disease before their contact with Europeans, since (and note now his exact words) "they had not yet tasted the sweet diet of civilization." Twenty years have passed and this Johnny-come-lately now also claims that the pre-Columbian ornament which the original report said had been clamped around the forearm of one of the skeletons just happened to be lying there beside these primitive blacks and was therefore "an accidental association".

But the matter does not end there. When I visited the Virgin Islands in 1976 to investigate this matter, I was led to a waterfall at St. John's, not far from where the skeletons were found. My guides thought that the carving of certain tropical animals on the rocks might be significant but that was of no consequence. As I approached the basin of the fall, however, the water reflected a dot and crescent formation on the lower face of the rock. I spent a day, up to my waist in water, laboriously chalking all the depressions in the rockpool at Reef Bay. For two years after that I sent this around to several people. Someone identified it as the Gye Nyame sign but that proved to be false. Eventually Dr. Barry Fell of Harvard claimed it was the Tifinagh branch of the Libyan script, a script not only used by some Libyans but a people of medieval Mali. Fell had come under attack for some of his translations and so I sent it for corroboration to the Libyan Department of Antiquities. They came up with roughly the same translation: "Plunge in to cleanse impurity. This is water for purification before prayer."

But there are more linguistic connections. I had mentioned the gold-tipped spears that Columbus testified had been brought to Haiti by "black-skinned people." I had mentioned also that metallurgical assays in Spain showed that they were identical with the spears forged in African Guinea. Now look closely at the words, the sounds, that both Africans and Americans were using to refer to them. Africans were using *ghana, kane, kanine, ghanin* and the native Americans repeated these sounds, revising them ever so slightly to suit their own tongue. Thus we have among the native Americans, *goana, caona, guani, guanin.* They also added a new word—*guanini*—to refer to the African gold merchants.

There is also botanical evidence—that is, evidence of the crossing of plants from Africa to America and from America to Africa. In South America before Columbus we have evidence of the cross-over of an Old World plant—the banana. Now the banana is not African. Africans did not have bananas originally. The Arabs introduced a specific banana into Africa and the Africans gave it a specific name. They called it *ba-ko-ko.* I have gone through half a dozen South American languages, tracking down the African ba-ko-ko word. It would be very difficult to deny an African connection. In the South American language Galibi we find the African banana word baccuccu, in the Oyapock language, the banana word baco; in Oyampi, the word *bacome*, in Tupi the word *pacoba*, in Apiacas, the word *pacowa*, in Puri the word *bahoh*, and in Coroada, the word *bacoeng*. One thing is clear. There was no native South American banana. That has been very clearly established. Its appearance in pre-Spanish Peruvian graves and its African-related names cannot be explained by an introduction after Columbus.

There is also evidence in the form of a map which as early as 1448—roughly half a century before Columbus—shows both the outlines of Brazil as well as the relatively exact distance of Brazil from the West African coast. So there you have it—eyewitness accounts, metallurgical evidence, linguistic evidence, botanical evidence, cartographic evidence (the map) oceanographic evidence (the currents that sweep you from Africa to America) skeletal, oral, documented, and above all, iconographic evidence—that is, paintings and sculptures of these people which show clearly, except to those who refuse to see, all the features we associate with the African. There is also, as I mentioned, the epigraphic evidence, (that is, the script I found on the rock at St John's in the U.S. Virgin Islands).

DBJ: What about the boats they came in? Tarzan movies give millions of people the impression that African navigational development stopped at the canoe.

IVS: Both ancient and medieval African boats have been tested on the Atlantic sea routes to America and crossed the ocean successfully. Thor Heyerdahl, with the help of Buduma boatmen on Lake Chad, rebuilt a pre-Christian African craft—a papyrus reed boat—and crossed the Atlantic successfully. Hannes Lindemann discovered that Africans had enormous dugouts as large as Viking ships. Lindemann tested one of these and made it to America in 52 days, 12 days less than Amerigo Vespucci, even though Vespucci left from an equally favorable starting point on the African-Atlantic coast. Dr. Alain Bombard rode a liferaft *L'Heretique* from Casablanca in North Africa via the Canaries to Barbados in 1952 without stocking up with adequate supplies of food and water, with only a cloth net for small sea fauna, a fishing line with hook for tunny, and two spears. He also carried a container for collecting water when rain fell. He survived in perfect health.

DG: Apart from the medieval journeys, you have presented a great deal of evidence for journeys long before Christ.

IVS: Yes, yes. That is the most important section of my new book—the section on the Olmec. The Olmec is the first major civilization in America.

DG: Your critics claim that you said African-Egyptians founded the Olmec civilization.

IVS: That is a naked and nasty lie. I have never said so. The native Americans created their own civilization. I pointed to contact with Old World peoples, in this case, the Egypto-Nubian. I demonstrated a number of remarkable coincidences between their ritual complexes and even a few of their technological developments. I spoke of an influence. All contacts between two peoples lead to influences. But I never claimed they brought civilization to Americans. That is a very Eurocentric type of claim. I pointed to specific elements in Nile Valley civilization (both Egyptian and Nubian) which are found as early as the era of Ramses III (c. 1200 B.C.) and persist in Nile Valley civilization even beyond the eighth century B.C., era of the Nubian renaissance.

DG: You mention a number of remarkable coincidences between the ritual complex of the Egypto-Nubian and the Olmec and you say there is clear evidence of their antecedence in the Egypto-Nubian world. Would you cite some of these?

IVS: In my new book I cite a dozen of these. Science requires only eight. When it can be shown that there are only four such coincidences between Chinese and native American complexes it is considered enough to establish a contact. My thesis presents the eight required, plus an extra four. But that is not enough where people from the African continent is concerned. It is dismissed as Afrocentric fantasy and "feel-good" therapy.

DG: Would you cite some of these.

IVS: The Egyptians have a double crown, for example. In addition to that, they have a bird and serpent motif on the crown.

DG: Why?

IVS: The *double-crown* represents *the two lands they controlled*: Egypt and Nubia. Also the Pharaoh was considered the representative of God, controlling both the upper and lower worlds. *The bird* represented *the upper world* and *the serpent the lower*. We find this unique ritual complex among the Olmec—double crowns with the bird and serpent motif. It has a clear antecedence in the Egypto-Nubian world. It meets all the criteria required for positing an influence. Antecedence, uniqueness, complexity. If we find this in Europe or Asia, no problem, especially if they have the ships that could cross the ocean, which the Africans did. The Egyptians not only had that. They had a religious myth that energized them—a myth about the underworld at the Far West of their world. Also they have left a pre-Christian map showing the Atlantic coastlines of both Africa and part of the Americas— including the Gulf of Mexico and the upper half of South America. This map displays the correct latitudinal and longitudinal coordinates between the two continents, something not achieved again until two hundred years after Columbus.

DG: Okay, let us say it's a given that Egyptians and Nubians were here. Now it seems that whenever you have heard about transcontinental contact between the Europeans and folks in this hemisphere, there has been slaughter, genocide, slavery, and various kinds of horrors. How did the Africans relate to the indigenous people?

IVS: Well there are no books written at that time that tell us about their relationship but we do know in a much later period (and this has nothing to do with the Olmecs) we have isolated feuding between the two. We have evidence of this in Panama, for example, but that is post-Columbian. It is noted by Balboa. Much later, however, we have records of great friendships and alliances among them. You can see a picture of an African sitting as a chief among native American chiefs in that ground-breaking book, *The Red and the Black* by William Loren Katz.

DG: To come back to the unique and complex rituals you say are duplicated in the Olmec world and have clear antecedence in the Egypto-Nubian. Would you cite one or two more of these?

IVS: In the ancient Egyptian world, when a person of note dies, he is mummified and placed in a sarcophagus. There is a hole in the sarcophagus and a symbolic bird is sometimes drawn above the sarcophagus that is supposed to take the soul of the deceased and fly out with it through the hole. This bird has the face of a human. All these elements—the sarcophagus, the hole, the bird with human head—they are all found among the Olmec. Once again, something unique, found nowhere else in the world except in the Egypto-Nubian complex. It meets all the scientific criteria required to claim a possible influence. *Antecedence, uniqueness, complexity!* Again, in Nubia, we have human-headed coffins. They appear nowhere else in the world except among the Olmec. Again, in Egypt, there is a winged god, called Sokar. He's standing on the back of a snake, holding up his wings. Note all the details. This snake not only has a head where his head should be but a head where his tail should be. This is incredibly unique and nowhere else does this complex appear except in ancient Egypt. Its antecedence in Egypt is indisputable. Yet we find every detail of this unique ritual complex duplicated in America.

DG: What of the Olmec stone heads?

IVS: About a dozen of these have been found. Now, I want to make it clear at the outset of this discussion that not all of these are foreign types. I lived among the native Americans for the first twelve years of my life. I know them better than my own nuclear family, half of whom I never saw again after my babyhood, not until the teen years of my life. De Montellano, chief of my critics, claims that *all* the stone heads are "spitting images of the native American." I do not like to attack my critics personally. Arguments should be met with arguments. But I have to say in this case, this man is either blind or a bigot. Apart from the unique combination of nose, cheek, jaw, lips, there is one unhelmeted head with a tuft of Africoid hair and another one with seven braids. They are very realistically portrayed in spite of their size. As the head of the first American expedition Dr. Stirling said of the first stone head he examined: "Despite its great size, the workmanship is delicate and sure, the proportions perfect. Unique in character among aboriginal American sculptures, it is remarkable for its realistic treatment. The features are bold and amazingly negroid." He got into big trouble with his colleagues for saying that.

DG: Unbelievable.

IVS: Not only that. Here comes our infamous detractor, Bernard Ortiz de Montellano, "the little man with the big name," claiming that these stone heads only seemed to be of "black" people because they were made of dark volcanic stone. Then he goes on to say that they sometimes used white stone but it turned black over time. Still not sure that he is going to get over with that, he claims that they could not be modelled on Egyptians or Nubians because all ancient Egyptians and Nubians had "long, narrow noses" and that "short, flat noses are confined to the West African ancestors of African-Americans."

DG: I've heard enough. Who in the archeological establishment supported you?

IVS: The only one who is old enough and free of the constraints of his earlier position to tell it like it is, to speak the truth without fear or favor. Dr. Clarence Weiant! He actually headed the first expedition of the Smithsonian into the Olmec world. Dr. Matthew Stirling was delayed, I was told, for some reason, and Dr. Weiant was the first to head the American archeological team into this area. The *New York Times* it seemed trusted no one here in America to talk about this matter. When my book came out they called on a hyper-isolationist, Glyn Daniel, from Britain (mind you, not America) to give me a good thrashing. When Daniel submitted his attack they had to send it back and ask him to be more specific. He just ranted and raved against everything I had said. His negrophobic rage made it difficult for him to provide specific counter-arguments to my thesis. My informant told me that they had to send the critique back to England and ask him to be more specific. It was a vicious tirade. Everything I had said was a lie, a fantasy, an invention. Then I sent a letter of defence which was abbreviated and doctored but at least they published it. I heard that nearly 70 professors, people I don't know, wrote in my defence. None of their letters were published. It was the most voluminous response to a critique since the poet Robert Frost was attacked. But then came the most surprising thing of all. Dr. Clarence Weiant, who, I was made to understand, actually preceded the head of the first expedition in the field, Dr. Stirling, wrote the *Times* in my defence. Let me quote what he said about my work.

"As someone who has been immersed in Mexican archeology for some 40 years, and who participated in the excavation of the first of the giant heads, I must confess that I for one am thoroughly convinced of the soundness of Van Sertima's conclusions."

BG: So this is a generation later and you're still being attacked.

IVS: It is fiercely resisted because to revise the vision of Africa you have to revise the curriculum.

DG: When I was growing up and going to school this was not even thought about. The only history of Africans was the history of slavery. So how would you revise the curriculum? If you were in charge of the history curriculum of the New York public schools, what would you do?

IVS: Well I do not have the expertise or the time to revise a curriculum. What I have been doing as editor and publisher of the *Journal of African Civilizations* and what my wife, Jacqueline, has been doing, as editor of my many lectures(the best of which she tapes for public circulation) is to make students and teachers aware of the greatest achievements of Africans and African-Americans. A concentration on slavery and the history of the black struggle has a vital role in that but it should not be exclusive. It may produce angry and gallant freedom-fighters but not necessarily constructive builders. Beyond the horror and degradation of the past, there is the need to feel the pride and power of past achievement. I know that from my own life. First year at university, just studying primitives, I tried to kill myself. I only began to want to live again when I saw the other faces, felt the other forces of my history. Both the light and the dark are necessary. It is not a matter of "feeling good," but *"feeling whole"* through the recovery of the half-buried heart of our history.

DG: How can parents turn their children on to this material and make them more receptive to it?

IVS: I don't have all the answers to that David. But my wife and I are engaged at the moment in a really exciting project that could prove helpful to parents and teachers alike. We opened a school for the

Journal of African Civilizations, which, as you know, I edit and publish. We invite groups from each borough in New York. We bus them to the school. It's not far from our home. We serve refreshments at the lectures. I probe in depth the subject matter of each journal and we have a question-and-answer session. So far we've had three very successful sessions and we intend to have at least three in the coming year.

BG: There are schoolteachers in Brooklyn and now in Harlem who use our paper in their classrooms. It is very important to me that you talk a little bit about your childhood. Because if there is a junior high school teacher or elementary school student who is reading this, I'd like them to feel some connection with you. I'd like you to talk a little bit about your childhood.

IVS: Well, my childhood was very strange (as I said before) because the first divorce in the history of my country was the divorce between my mother and father. And the first remarriage recorded was between my mother and father. My father was an unusual man. He came third in the British world in a difficult empire-wide exam in Greek. He became superintendent over road and river transport in the heavily forested interior of Guyana. I grew up there in my childhood and when the divorce split my family apart I grew up with my father and elder brother. A native American woman became my foster mother. The forest zone was struck by a great disease—malaria. There was a deadly mosquito called the *anopheles*. Fifty percent of the people in that area died. Half of my friends died. I was dying at the age of nine. The doctors told my father there was no point saving my life because the fever had damaged my brain. I would not be much good to myself and a burden on him and everyone if I recovered. My father cried bitterly but he called in the priest to say the last rites. The priest sprinkled holy water on me and the water was so cold and I was so hot that the shock woke me up. But they were right. I did suffer permanent damage. They do say now in hospitals that up to a certain age the brain repairs itself. But I was beyond that age.

JVS: The brain creates new engrams, so it's possible that it seems to be repairing itself. It's not. It's taking a new route.

IVS: So, perhaps, it remained damaged. The thing that saved my life was my father, who, seeing me so depressed, said to me. "Ivan, even if you only have half a brain left, most people on this planet do not use half a brain. So if you use yours well you'll be ahead." That saved my life. And he gave me cards. This became very important to me because I still use them. He gave me large cards and he said to me. "Every day you fill a card with six facts and you must photograph it." I said to him, "But Daddy, we don't even have a camera." "Everything," he said, "everything that the human invents, whether it is a plane or a camera, starts in the head. So you are to pretend you have a camera in your head. Blink and blink again like you're photographing your card and you'll master the facts you put down on it. It will take time, it will take time, Ivan. It will take practice. But you will do it." I began to remember far more than other people because they weren't doing that, because they didn't have my problem and they didn't feel it was necessary to correct or complete themselves. I must confess I still have one or two problems to this day. I have to shake my hand in order to tell right from left. I cannot do it automatically. I'm lucky that my wife sits beside me in the motor car because I can't find my way back easily unless it is a straight road. Once I turn, I have to map it. It's not automatic. Because of the necessity to write things down I learned far more facts than most people. So it seems like a marvellous memory. It is not. It's a reconstructed memory.

DG: You said earlier to me "these are dark days" but you've been there before. When you were that young student facing British authority figures, and thinking, 'Wait a minute. I think something else, but there is all of this power around me that says I'm wrong'. Now, after all these years, after all the scholarship, after all your studies, aren't you able to respond to them better?

IVS: Yes, personally, but you see the thing that is bothering me is that these people have the power to sabotage my work. For example, they're campaigning for a withdrawal of my books from the schools, claiming that these things are falsehoods and shouldn't be taught.

DG: They're more desperate now because they know they are dealing with a more educated group of people. Not just you, Ivan. We're coming in numbers now.

IVS: Thank God one is not alone.

DG: To think that after all these years and all the work you've done, these people are still trying to sabotage you. You defended yourself eloquently before the Smithsonian, you appeared before a Congressional Committee and got them to delete the word "discovery," decisively debunking the Columbus myth. You sat on the Nobel Committee of the Swedish Academy for five years to advise on the selection of Nobel laureates in Literature. You were even invited to join UNESCO. You are the compiler of the first Swahili Dictionary of Legal Terms. You have edited twelve anthologies on African civilizations. Your poems appear in English, French and German anthologies. Yet there is a raging debate over everything you have written. They are still trying to put you down.

IVS: Well, fighting for a new vision of man, a new vision of history, is worth it, painful though it may be. The warrior's courage does not protect him from the wound of bullets.

But I have found over time that the negatives have been my greatest help. That is the one lesson I have learned over the years. The negative is very important. Oftentimes it is more important than the positive. Sometimes if something is highly successful and meets no great opposition, it can make you facile. If it meets with great negatives it can be even better in the end. Unless it is destroyed, it is far better that it meets with negatives. The negative makes you go back and check out everything. You find a whole lot of new things. If before you came in with a revolver, the next time you come in with a cannon. The time after that, you come in with a nuclear bomb.

On the Find of Nicotine in the Mummy of Ramses II

DIOP TO VAN SERTIMA

The following letter which appears in vol. 1, no. 2, of the *Journal of African Civilizations* (November 1979) is reprinted for the benefit of readers who would like to follow the discussion but have not seen the earlier correspondence.

Dakar
July 17, 1979

Dear Professor Van Sertima,

I received the issue of your Journal which you were so kind to send. I would like to call your attention to a fact which seems to specifically confirm your ideas on the African presence in pre-Columbian America.

The laboratories of Paris which have just analyzed the mummy of Ramses II have found nicotine (tobacco alkaloid) in his stomach. This nicotine served as treatment against the numerous cavities found in the teeth of the old pharoah.

Interestingly, most scholars support the fact that tobacco is a plant of American origin which had been introduced in Africa at a date that remains to be specified. Raymond Mauny thinks that this introduction could hardly be dated before the 16th century.

The first conclusion that one can obtain from these facts is the following: If tobacco is really a plant of American origin, the nicotine in the stomach of the mummy of Ramses II is irrefutable proof that the contacts between Africa and America go back to at least 1300 years before Christ in the middle of the historical period of Egypt; and many historical facts and pre-Columbian civilizations would find there the beginning of an explanation. You probably are already aware of this fact.

In my next letter, I will send you the details and references needed, but I am going away tomorrow and I wanted to send you this information before my departure. I will be returning to Dakar in three weeks

In my works entitled "L'Afrique Noire pre-Coloniale" (Pre-Colonial Black Africa) and "'Antiquité Africaine par l'image" (African Antiquity through Images), I dealt with the possibilities of pre-Columbian contacts between Africa and America but it was only a working hypothesis. Thus you can imagine how much pleasure your discoveries gave me, because of the conclusive evidence they constitute for historical science. All my congratulations!

It should be noted that the analysis carried out on the mummy of Ramses II has a tendentious aspect that I have taken upon myself to refute in the chapter of a general work which is about to be published. In effect, the authors wanted discreetly to "whiten" the mummy. They have tried vainly to present Ramses II as white-skinned.

Sincerely yours,

Cheikh Anta Diop
Director, Radio Carbon Laboratories
IFAN Institute, University of Dakar

VAN SERTIMA TO DIOP

(Reply to letter published in vol. 1, no. 2 *Journal of African Civilizations* issue)

Dr. Cheikh Anta Diop,
Directeur du Laboratoire
   du Radiocarbone
IFAN Institute, Université de Dakar
Dakar, SENEGAL   August 22, 1979

Dear Professor Diop,

I had not replied to your letter of July 17 before because I was waiting to receive the details on the tobacco find which you had promised to send me on your return to Dakar. I dispatched a cable to you a day or two ago and am writing you now in the hope that my letter may expedite your response. I await the details of the evidence on tobacco.

The problem of tobacco in the Old and New Worlds is more complex than would at first appear. I am sending you a photostat of my chapter on the matter—chapter 2 "Smoking, Tobacco and Pipes" (pp. 207-231) which I hope you will examine closely at your convenience. In this chapter I use primary sources initially examined by Leo Wiener, a Harvard linguist, in the 1920s , but I subject his source materials to a critical analysis which has led me to very different conclusions. As you will see from my analysis, there is the possibility of both an indigenous American and an indigenous African brand of tobacco. The word "tubbaq" derives from the Syrian word "dubbaq" (viscum, glue) a word that suggests the nature of the substance that issues from the plant. It is mentioned in early Moorish treatises on agriculture. It referred initially, however, to a variety of viscous substances used in fumigation of patients ("smoking-out" cures), We do not know exactly when it came to be used for the tobacco plant, as such. It appears that the Africans did have a tobacco plant and added uses—magical, meditative and medicinal—which were later found duplicated in America. There is no evidence that the Africans introduced tobacco into America (as Wiener claims) but they certainly introduced certain ritual and medicinal and meditative practices associated with the "tubbaq" or tabaco. The Americans did not have a word for the tobacco plant that was anywhere close to tabaco. They only used the word *tabaco* to refer to the "act of smoking" and the "instrument for smoking" (the pipe) some types of which were introduced by the Africans. Several smoke-words in America, apart from *tabaco,* have great antiquity in Africa (Malinke words like *dyamba, dyemba* and Toma and Bambara words like *duli* which have their variants *nduli* and *luli* in Mende) Wiener mapped the distribution of these words in America in the medieval period with great skill. He was a brilliant linguist but very weak in presentation of his evidence in a logical and analytical manner that would meet our more rigorous standards of scholarship, jumping to conclusions which his evidence could not support.

It is quite possible, as you suggest, that an early visit by Egyptians to America led to the importation of the tobacco plant into Africa and that the African tubbaq is a derivative of the American, borrowed and cultivated in a pre-Columbian period. To establish this, however, one would have to subject the tobacco found in the belly of Ramses II to a chemical, and probably to a botanical, analysis to determine whether it *is* "American" tobacco. The assumption that tobacco is an exclusive American indigene is simply that—an assumption. We are, therefore, in a dilemma unless further revelatory details are forthcoming.

There is no doubt, however, as a result of this find, that the use of tobacco in Africa is of great antiquity and it certainly strengthens the case for the introduction of "smoking practices" and the "smoke-words" associated with those practices, to the American, through later pre-Columbian voyages by Africans. The evidence, therefore, even though it may not be regarded, in itself or by itself, as indisputable proof of a pre-Columbian contact between Africa and America in *the era of the Ramessids,* would place the discussion of tobacco in a revolutionary context and lead to a reexamination of this whole issue, which I would welcome.

By the way, although I have presented evidence in my book for Egypto-Nubian voyages in the first millenium B.C. and Leo Wiener (1920-22) and later Rogers (1942) and Harold Lawrence (1963) etc. have argued (or outlined some of the arguments) for Mandingo voyages in the medieval period (which I also develop in my book) there is hard evidence for a much earlier contact in the period of the Ramessids, which fits in with this extraordinary find. R. A. Jairazbhoy, in his book *Ancient Egyptians and Chinese in America (1974)* deals with this thesis very persuasively although I have found him to be so radically diffusionist that he sometimes ruins his case through over-statement.

I am very keen to continue this correspondence and look forward to hearing from you. With your permission I would like to publish our dialogue in the *Journal of African Civilizations.* I would also like to extend to you from the Directors of the Journal our very best wishes. We would like to regard you as our Overseas Editor or Editorial Adviser in Africa and would publish anything in this field which you recommend to us. We regard you as the leading light in the world at the moment working for a change of consciousness with regard to the history and culture of African peoples.

Yours, in brotherhood,

Ivan Van Sertima

P.S. A French edition of my book will be available from *EDITIONS FLAMMARION (Paris)* sometime in 1980. In the meantime I am sending an autographed copy of the English edition of the book by separate mail.

EDITOR'S NOTE

After a long delay and a cable and phone call to Dakar, Senegal, which received no response, my letter of August 22 was followed by a note to Diop in which I offered to withdraw from the debate and let his letter on the subject (published in vol. 1, no. 2—November 1979) stand as the last word. It is to this note that Dr. Diop refers when he speaks of my "unilaterally abandoning discussion out of tact" and advises me against "any concession when it is a question of establishing a scientific truth."

DIOP TO VAN SERTIMA

Dakar, November 26, 1979

Dr. Cheikh Anta Diop
Directeur du Laboratoire de Radiocarbone
  de l'IFAN,
Université de Dakar, Senegal

Professor Van Sertima	*Note*: (Readers should *not*
59 South Adelaide Avenue	use this address. Editor
Highland Park, New Jersey 08904	left this address in 1984.)

Your two letters are a great reassurance to me because they indicate that we now have young Afro-American scholars of international stature, thoroughly devoted to historic research. I assure you that there was no misunderstanding. You had understood exactly the import of my letter. Your sense of decorum does you credit, but it ought not induce you to unilaterally abandon discussion out of tact, and thereby to sacrifice scientific truth. Once again, this very African comportment delights me and even more gratifying is the concern for precision, conveyed by your last letter. Remember that we are focused on a quest for truth and not on a sacrosanct idol whom we have to avoid debasing. So, there shouldn't be any concession when it is a question of establishing a scientific truth, and I urge you to publish in its entirety your last letter to me, without which, otherwise, this letter would be incomprehensible.

The problem of the origin of tobacco probably is not yet resolved, though authors such as A. L. Guyot, Raymond Mauny, and certainly others rely on a variety of aruguments to assert American origin of that plant.[1] Several of these authors are honest scholars, motivated only by the desire to establish a scientific truth, useful to the research on this subject, but others whose ideologies show partiality are prevented from attaining scientific truth in spite of their technical competence; these last often are motivated only by the desire to divest Africa of everything, even of her botanical heritage, if I may say so. Thus, R. Mauny is committing a subtle error in confusing, in the text which I have cited, the origin of tobacco and the use of the pipe. The comments included in my first letter therefore were intended for these two categories of authors who for diverse reasons postulate South American origin of tobacco. Acceptance of their premise would mean that *if* tobacco really is a plant of American origin taking into account the presence of nicotine in the stomach of Rameses II, one has to assume that Egypto-American relations existed under the 19th dynasty, 1300 years before Christ.

In fact nicotine[2] is the principal and specific alkaloid of tobacco. All varieties of tobacco contain it, the percentage varying only with the species. The other alkaloidal plants such as the sleep-inducing poppy, the coffee-tree, etc., contain other alkaloids, entirely different

---

1.   Raymond Mauny, Tableau Geographique de l'quest Africain au Moyen-Age. 1961. Collection "Memoires de l'IFAN" n 61. p. 59:
      "Pipes are one of the most useful West African "fossil directors": their presence dates them to a period after 1600 and, in nearly every case in Muslim territory, before 1900. The arrival date of tobacco, an American plant, is in fact well-known: the Tarikh-el-Fettach teaches us that the use of that plant for smoking was introduced to Timbuktu (Tombouctou) between 1594 and 1596, and from 1600 onwards, it was observable on the African coasts."
      A. L. Guyot. Origine des Plantes cultivées. 1942. Presses Universitaires de France. Collection que sais-je? p. 69:
      "The Pacific coast of South America is another important center of origin for cultivated species: even more than the hot and humid tropical plains, the unscathed slopes of the Andean Cordilleras were, from the outset, inhabited by man. Originating from here are: tobacco. tomatoes, beans, potatoes: . . . but. . . . "
      A. L. Guyot was a professor at L'École Nationale d'Agriculture de Grignon in France in 1942.
2.   The chemical formula of nicotone is: $C_{10}H_{14}N_2$ which is diagrammed overleaf:

from nicotine, although capable of producing narcotic effects that are similar or more intense and more toxic to the organism. Therefore, the presence of nicotine necessarily indicates the use of a variety of true tobacco and not simply of a related plant that inappropriately could bear that name. Tobacco must have been used throughout antiquity in human and veterinary medicine, as you have shown, before its use for smoking was practiced.

Modern methods of chemical analysis afford detection of the nicotine molecule when that substance is present in even an infinitesimal quantity; confirmation from the analyses in Paris would prove, therefore, that the Egyptians were familiar with tobacco as early as 1300 B.C., even though they did not smoke it, for one does not find representation of the pipe on the pharaonic monuments. This would disprove the contention that tobacco was introduced in Africa in a post-columbian period. Even if exclusively indigenous to America, tobacco would have been introduced in Africa as early as the 19th Egyptian dynasty, coming after maritime contact; unless one supposes, as others have tried to do, the accidental arrival of the seeds of various plants on the African coasts by means of floatation on the sea's surface and by force of the tides: a hypothesis that is more than hazardous and not a little improbable which we pose only to cover all sides of the question. (See diagram)

There remains your hypothesis, expressed in your letter of August 22, 1979, namely: an innate origin of tobacco both in Africa and in America; I cannot evaluate this particular proposition at this point in the research. If it were thus, the presence of nicotine in the stomach of Rameses II would not prove pre-columbian, Afro-american contact and you certainly are right in making this very important observation. In this case, there would have been parallel usage of tobacco in Africa

Diagram for the chemical formula of nicotine ($C_{10}H_{14}N_2$).

and America, and the only new element would be the certainty which we now have of the use of tobacco in Africa as early as the 19th dynasty, therefore, since antiquity.

What remains to be seen now is whether the species that could be considered indigenous to Africa are true tobaccos, containing nicotine, those which you mention in your letter, for example: *dyamba* or *dyemba* in Malinke, etc. Indeed, we have in Walaf (Wolof), a Senegalese language, the same root as in Malinke: *yambass,* designating an alkaloidal plant that is a true drug, even more toxic than nicotine, which is smoked like tobacco. It is an Indian hemp, a narcotic plant and a substitute for opium. This plant is being studied by a team in the department of pharmacy of Dakar and I will try to specify the particular alkaloid it contains in another letter.

To my knowledge, the fifty-two Parisian laboratories have not yet published the results of their analyses of the mummy of Rameses II, and it is for this reason that we cannot yet present anything with certainty except the discovery of nicotine: this is certain. As soon as anything new on this subject is published, I will inform you of it.

Please accept my regards, Professor.

Cheikh Anta Diop

(Translated from the French for publication by Rosanne Harris)

Notes on Correspondences between Ancient Egyptian and Ancient Mexican Pyramids

Bart Jordan was a child prodigy to whom Einstein granted special audience because of his phenomenal mathematical abilities. He has shown extraordinary correspondences between ancient Egyptian and ancient American pyramids. We present below a contribution by this remarkable genius on unsuspected correspondences between Old World/ New World pyramids.

The measures of the monuments in both the New World and the Old World share common features which are currently missed by investigators. The problem stems from having misread the units of measures and their specific settings. The basis for the Great Pyramid of Giza, Jordan shows, was specifically the synodical revolution of Venus: 583.921 x 10 = 5839.21 inches high Some years ago Jordan visited the ancient New World site of Chaco Canyon. While he was there he measured a monument called Wijiji and found it to have a perimeter of precisely 584 feet. This, he shows, was clearly a reference to synodical Venus and because earlier investigators had measured it in meters, the meaning of the monument was lost. He shows . that "the calendrical data incorporated into the measures had to be very exacting, too exacting to be invented a second time".

I present his extraordinary essay below. I have taken the liberty of summarizing it above for those who do not understand mathematics.

"The measures of the monuments in both the New World and the Old World share common features which are currently missed by investigators. The problem stems from having misread the units of measures and their specific settings. The basis for the Great Pyramid at Giza, for example, was specifically the synodical revolution of Venus 553.921 x 10 = 5839.21 inches high.

$$1$$
$$21$$
$$321$$
$$4321$$
$$54321$$
$$\underline{654321}$$
$$713306$$

"The inch of the pyramid was the inch as we know it. The inch was the basis of the cubits in the ancient world. So was the meter. R. J. Gillings, in his *Mathematics in the Time of the Pharaohs*, wrote: "A *cubit* was originally the length of a forearm, from the elbow to the tip of the middle finger. Of course, the limbs of individuals varied in length and two standard cubits came into common use early, the *royal cubit* and the *short cubit*. The former was the cubit usually used for measurement in everyday life and was 20.6 inches (more accurately 20.59), while the short cubic is reckoned to be 17.72 inches, hence the "cubit and a hand's breadth."

In a footnote, Gillings refers to Sir Alan Gardiner's value of 0.523 meter or 20.59 inches for the royal cubit. My investigation showed the value to be 0.52311 meter or 20.59463 inches. My investigation of one short cubit rendered the value of 17.718 inches. These cubits had different names which referred to their values. The royal cubit was the *music cubit* and the short cubit was the *lunar cubit*. The music cubit was derived from 10 plus (10 x 1,059463, the twelfth root of two). 1.059463 separates each semitone from every other semitone in the music scale. The lunar cubit was 354.36 divided by 20.

Values given in inches have meaning. All the monuments need to be reexamined before we will know what the ancients were trying to preserve by their measures. The music cubit, for example, took 1 + 059 + 463 = 523 as the metric base. It appended 11 to the figure to commemorate the 11 semitones within the octave and the 11 days difference between the 365-day solar year and the 354-night lunar year. The total figure was 0.52311 meter. Incidentally, the *Solar Cubit* was 18.628 inches or 365.24 divided by 20. It differed from the *Light Cubit* of 18.628 inches by 0.366 or leap year.

365.24 – 354.36 = 10.88; the speed of sound is 1088 feet per second. The speed of sound had to be determined before the speed of light. Eventually, (1088 x 904012) + 208 = 983565264 or 528 x 1862813 was derived by the ancients. This footage was matched by the figure of 2997925 hectometers. The measures were then encoded as follows: the 2997925 hectometers as 2 + 997 + 925 = 1924 and the 1862813 statustades as 1 + 862 + 313 = 1676 came to 3600 or 60 x 60. One is reminded here of 60 seconds x 60 minutes. In any event, 1924 x 1676 = 3224624; that is 1059463 + 1059463+ 1059463 + 46235 (semitone scale of 4 South 6 West 2 Center 3 East 5 North). Here then is the ultimate basis for the music scale with its rainbow colours of Red Orange Yellow Green Blue predicated on light.

To return to the royal or music cubit and the short or lunar cubit. 20.59463 – 17.718 = 2.87663. This interval contains the following figures: 2.35604 (day) + 0.46235 (scale) + 0.05280 (mile) + 0.00544 (sound). Also, the solar cubit of 18.262 – the lunar cubit of 17.718 = 0.544. Note that 0.544 x 2000 = 1088, echoing the speed of sound.

Two cubits worth noting are a *Phobos and Deimos cubit* of 22.77150 and a *flood date cubit* of 21.7600 (Flood at 2nd month, 17th day, and 600th year). 22,77150 – 0.00087 (synodical Mars mirrored) – 2. 17600 = 20.59463 *music cubit*. The music scale to which the cubit refers comes from 8765 – 4321 or 4444. The Fundamental Tone is 44.44 exactly. The list of nine overtones paired with the "begat years" of Adam to Noah culminates in the figure 243723. Witness that Mars rotates in 24n37m23s. The ancient world has some truly remarkable measures.

Altering the inches, feet, and meter by the twelfth root of two is not only limited to the Old World. The New World monuments, many examined by Hugh Harleston, have employed a 1.059463 meter. Until investigators measure with a perseverance and carefulness that attends his work, measures will continue to go unrecorded as to their specific intent. This is the situation as I see it. I can only hope that this brief commentary on the ancient measures will spark some effort into re-covering the lost material.

I began this commentary with a measurement of the Great Pyramid at Giza. I showed it to be based on measures relating to Venus. That was the Old World. Some years ago, I visited the ancient New World site of Chaco Canyon. While I was there, I measured a monument called Wijiji and found it to have a perimeter of precisely 584 feet:

$$10.66 \times 16 = 170.56$$
$$10.88 \times 11 = 119.68$$
$$10.88 \times 11 = 119.68$$
$$10.88 \times 16 = 174.08$$

Clearly the measure or 584 feet was a reference to synodical Venus. The building was measured by the investigators in meters; hence, the meaning of the monument was lost. Many other measures of the Chaco system are misread. This is a great pity as it is a most remarkable site.

There is much to do and cooperation between Old World and New World investigators is absolutely essential, especially where contact and influence are suspected. My examination of the cubits is a case in point. There was a very exacting science which led to their use in the construction of the edifices. I have tried to give some clarification to the process behind the measurements in order to show that the calendrical data incorporated into *the measures had to be very exacting, too exacting to be invented a second time.* The information contained in the measures had to be carried and duplicated from generation to generation. What we have to do now is put away our differences and search anew.

Bart Jordan

Notes on Correspondences between some Nubian and Mexican Pyramids

De Montellano et al. have also raised questions about the pyramids in Nubia, arguing that they were not stepped pyramids like some in the New World, that they only appear to be stepped. I present their argument below and Professor Lumpkin's reply.

Both Van Sertima (1976:132; 1992:12) and Beatrice Lumpkin (1992:145–46), one of his supporters, have argued that "some" of the Nubian pyramids of the eighth and seventh centuries B.C. were originally constructed as step pyramids. This assertion is quite doubtful; The pyramids in question (at Nuri; and El Kurru) are in a very bad state of repair, and it is difficult to make a judgment one way or another. A diagram of a "typical" Nubian pyramid that appears in Lumpkin (1992:146) seems to be stepped, but it also has a top that comes to a point. This suggests that the alleged "steps" had no functional purpose, which is the complete opposite of Mesoamerican practice. It also suggests what is much more probable: that the pyramids lost their outer casement or covering blocks that would have given them their smooth appearance in ancient times (see Edwards 1985; plate 35, or any other contemporary distant or close-up view of Khafre's pyramid at Giza, which has the remains of original casement blocks still situated at the top).

Professor Lumpkin's Reply

Dear Professor Van Sertima,

Thank you for informing me that a question has been raised as to whether some of the Nubian pyramids were step pyramids. May I refer again to the reference which I cited on this subject? It was *The Pyramids,* by the Egyptian Egyptologist, Ahmed Fakhry, 1969, 140-141. In his description of the pyramids of El Kurru he wrote, "Each had a superstructure built around a core of mud, sand, and small, rough pieces of stone, covered with a smooth or stepped sandstone casing. Again, in describing the pyramids of Nuri, Fakhry wrote, "Some are stepped; others have smooth casings." (Fakhry, 1969, 245.)

Also, the "functional purpose" of steps in a pyramid has been questioned in cases where the steps have been covered to create smooth sides and to allow the pyramid to rise to a point. I.E.S. Edwards, *The Pyramids of Egypt,* 1979, p.289, thought the steps, even though covered, retained their religious significance. Smith writes about the pyramid builders who built composite pyramids, and followed "the practice of superimposing the new type of tomb on the old (fig. 57) and thereby no doubt hoped to profit from the magical properties ascribed to both types."

Pyramids (3)—Norman Totten

When *They Came Before Columbus* was published in 1977, the *New York Times* critic, Glyn Daniel, launched a savage attack against my thesis. Among the things he said that were downright falsehoods was that the American pyramids were temples while the Egyptian pyramids were tombs. This is the sort of pseudo-scientific rubbish we get from our present critics who hide their ignorance behind academic degrees, often slavishly earned and proudly paraded by repeating facile falsehoods that have gained general acceptability.

With respect to the Glyn Daniel statement, I refer my readers to a letter by Dr. Norman Totten, archeologist-historian, who was site supervisor for the archeological excavation at Deir Alla, Jordan. The following is an excerpt from Dr. Totten's letter, which the *New York Times* would not publish in the heat of a controversy that brought more letters, says the *Washington Post,* than any critique since Robert Frost was attacked:

> Daniel states without qualification, to disprove possible linkage between Egyptian and American pyramids, that "American pyramids are temple platforms; the Egyptian pyramids are tombs". This is news to those of us who stood inside the tomb chambers of the great pyramids of Cuicuilco and Cholula, Mexico. It disregards the fact that the thousands of earthen pyramids across the United States were of two contemporaneous types, temple platforms and tombs. And what of the great stone Maya pyramid with its temple on top and famous tomb with sarcophagus within, the so-called "Temple of the Inscriptions" at Palenque"?
>
> While his understanding of American pyramids is erroneous, his statement about Egyptian pyramids is simplistic and misleading. Certainly the great pyramids at Sakkara, Giza, and Dashur were tombs. I have been inside a number of them. There were, however, funerary and valley temples adjoining those pyramids

as an integral part of their total plan. The sun temple of Pharaoh Ne-suer-ra (5th Dynasty) at Abusir had a huge kind of obelisk set on a pyramidal platform, and was not a burial chamber but a temple complex. The famous mortuary temple of Mentuhotep I, founder of the 11th Dynasty at Dier El Bahri, Thebes, was topped by a pyramid. (Letter to Van Sertima from Norman Totten published in *Journal of African Civilizations*, vol. 8, no. 2, 1986).

Pyramids (4)—Bart Jordan

Jose Arguelles compared the Cheops pyramid in Egypt with the Mexican pyramid at Palenque (see p. 78 of *The Mayan Factor: Path Beyond Technology*, 1987)

The birth date of Pacal Votan of Palenque, 13 66 560, has been shown to have a broad array of periodicities important to the Maya. The death date of 13 85 540 was also given. The difference between the two dates (1366560 and 1385540) is 18980 or 52 x 365. This 52-year span from birth to death was the *ritual life* of the ruler who then met his end voluntarily. This was an all important event. Arguelles may have missed the point of the dates because he failed to multiply them out as follows: 13 x 66 x 560 or 480480 and 13 x 85 x 540 or 596700. Adding (1366560 + 480480) + (1385540 + 596700) comes to 3829280, divisible by both 280 (gestation) and 260 (sacred cycle).

Then one adds all the numbers accordingly 1 + 3 + 6+ 6 + 5 + 6 + 0 plus 4+ 8 + 0+ 4 + 8 + 0 and 1 + 3 + 8 + 5 + 5 + 4 + 0 plus 5 + 9 + 6 + 7 +0 + 0, equalling 104 exactly. The 104 was divided by 4, coming to 26. Also, there are precisely 26 numbers in the calculation. The total of 3829280 plus 26 is 3829306 or 25920 + 1862813 + 25920 and 25920 + 1862813 + 25920. Precession of the equinoxes is 25920 years and the speed of light is 1862813 statustades or tenths of miles (528 feet) per second.

While precession of the equinoxes at 25920 was known to the Maya, the ancient calculation of the speed of light at 1862813 statustades was not. The information and measures were given to the Maya. The edifices at Palenque ought to be measured again with this information in hand.

Conversations with Von Wuthenau
(Mexico, 1985)

On the importance of the pictorial document in the face of an almost wholesale destruction of American books by order of the bigot Bishop de Landa:
"Burn them all. They are works of the Devil."

VAN SERTIMA:
May I interject here, Alex, to consolidate what you are saying because many people are not aware of the fact that it is necessary, far more necessary than in Europe, to concentrate on other areas of evidence than the written document. It is relatively easy for historians to reconstruct early passages of European history from the written document because Europe had the good fortune to maintain an archival continuity. In spite of all its wars, its libraries were not destroyed. Yet here, in America, as you have just pointed out, you have a virtual absence of documents. As in the case of Africa, (the university of Timbuctoo, for example), it was not the lack of writing as most people want to believe, but a destruction, an almost systematic destruction, of documents. One remembers the exhortation of that bigot, Bishop de Landa, ordering the destruction of native American books in the Yucatan. "Burn them all," he said, "they are works of the devil." So it has become necessary in the reconstruction of American history to concentrate on other areas of evidence and, as you say these figures, these faces, these human images, are witness to a whole sequence of ages, a whole sequence of cultures . . .

VON WUTHENAU:
More than that. They are portraits of the living by their contemporaries. No professor nowadays has seen a living Olmec. The carver of the Olmec saw these people and they are the ones who transmit the

Van Sertima and Von Wuthenau holding a discussion on pre-Columbian terracotta.

truth of the history. You cannot make up all these things in your imagination. It's impossible that all the differentiation of races which were so meticulously and precisely portrayed by the artist were never here. We are looking into the faces of actual people who lived here. That is why it is the backbone of our research into the ancient history of the whole American continent. Mexico is just a part of it . . .

Ignorance of the Surviving Pictorial Document as Displayed by Conventional Anthropologists

Comas (1973: 75–92) said there were no such Africoid figurines, that no image in American sculpture looked like anything other than the typical Mongoloid type that came across the Bering Straits from Asia. His latter-day disciple, de Montellano, agrees. They are all "spitting images of the native". Michael Coe told my interviewer, Boyce Rensberger, who did an essay on my book for the *Science Digest* in 1981, that he had never seen any terracotta figurines in Mexico that looked African. Apart from Negrophobic blindness, which is a common disease among many established anthropologists (I was trained by the most celebrated Negrophobics in the British empire) it may well be that he was never exposed to the range and variety of ancient American terracotta. The Museum of Anthropology in Mexico City, for example, displays less than half a dozen of these among their thousands of exhibits and the references to them are designed to give the public the impression that they are post-Columbian. Those who would like to hold on to this line of thinking should be forewarned that a few of these have been subjected to thermino-luminescence dating. Von Wuthenau's organization of these into specific time-frames or historical periods is not mere guesswork. It is based not only on stratigraphy and typology but, in some cases, on advanced methods of dating.

—From Van Sertima's Smithsonian Address, 1991.

Plants and Transplants

Botanists have provided further corroborative evidence. The Portuguese arrived in West Africa about 1450, possibly before. The Portuguese found a cotton growing plentifully in West Africa and they took this cotton and planted it in the Cape Verde islands in 1462—thirty years before Columbus. They assumed it to be indigenously African. Twentieth-century analyses have shown that it was not African at all. It was *Gossypium hirsutum var punctatum*, which was grown in the pre-Columbian Caribbean and in parts of South America. It is not African, yet it was transplanted to Africa and was growing plentifully there before Columbus (Stephens 1971:413). Not only that. *Zea mays* has been found in pre-Columbian Africa. American *Zea mays!* Professor M. D. W. Jeffreys of Witwaterstrand University, a South African linguist, showed how American maize had traveled to Africa. It is distinct from African sorghum. It had moved across the African continent and he traced it down through linguistic footprints. The Russians picked it up as it moved from Africa into Asia. Russian botanists identified it and showed that American *Zea mays* had entered Asia before the time of the Columbus voyages. All this we ignore.

On Columbus's third voyage also, when his ships landed on the northeastern coast of South America. his crewmen described a certain dress consisting of a material and design identical to the *almayzar* that the Portuguese found Africans wearing in Guinea (Thacher 1903:2:393). In South America, the European visitors also found plants brought in through earlier contacts. Take the banana! The banana is not African. It is an Asian cultigen. However, it was brought into Africa through trade and acquired a name associated with the Africans—*bakoko*, a name which has several near-identicals in South America. We found the medieval Peruvians digging up bodies and reburying them, feeding them symbolically with certain kinds of fruit. In the graves of the reburied dead, in late pre-Columbian strata in South America, we find the banana. The Arabs introduced the Asian banana in their trade with Africa from the twelfth century on. They took it out of Asia and introduced it to Africa. All the African, as well as the Arab-African, words for banana run through the South American languages in recognizable form. Consider, for example, the indigenous African word for banana unrelated to the more popular Arab-African word *platano* and *platena,* which had been introduced a century earlier into Spain through Moorish trade. The African word for banana is *bakoko.* In the South American language Galibi we find the word for banana is *baccuccu;* in the Oyapock language, *baco*; in Oyampi, *bacome*; in Tupi, *pacoba;* in Apiacas, *pacowa,* in Puri, *bahoh;* in Coroada, *bacoeng,* (Wiener 1922:2:130). There is also the plantain variety, the sister of the banana. The early sixteenth-century explorer Orellana tells us that he saw the plantain in ubiquitous cultivation along the Amazon (Van Sertima I976:199). But there was no native South American banana. That has been very clearly established. Its appearance in pre-Spanish Peruvian graves and the ubiquity of its sister, the plantain, along the Amazon in 1513 cannot be explained by an introduction after Columbus.

—From Smithsonian Address, 1991

Fade from Black—
The Significance of the Skeletal Evidence

Since in extreme instances, one race may fade into the other, in the sense of unusual types of one race having average characteristics of the other, a further close check has to be made to ensure that this possibility is not distorting the picture. In very mixed populations this would be a very difficult process open to much error, but in the dry areas of the Olmec civilization Wiercinski found clear evidence of a racial type different from that of the native population appearing as a significant minority. All the indices used to distinguish races through the study of surviving skulls and close comparison with skulls found in continental African and native American graveyards make it quite clear that a foreign racial element (African) entered the Olmec world at this time.

A number of extremely interesting facts emerged from a study of the skeletal evidence. *Wiercinski noted that 13.5 percent of the skeletons examined in the pre-Classic Olmec cemetery of Tlatilco were "Negroid" or "Africoid," yet only 4.5 percent of those found later at Cerro de las Mesas from the Classic period were.* This indicates that the African element intermingled until it almost fused with the native population. *Female skeletons found in the graves from the pre-Classic period, and lying side by side with African males, are racially distinct from them (that is, native American Females, foreign African males) but they appear racially similar to their male companions at a later "Classic" site, indicating progressive intermixture and the growing absorption of the foreign African element into the largely Mongoloid (Asiatic) American population.*

This makes it very clear that the Olmec-African element was a distinctive, outside injection that came and crossbred in the Olmec time period and that it did not represent "proto-Australoid" or "proto-

negroid" aborigines who trickled into America from the Pacific in the very ancient glacial epoch when the very first Americans came. According to Wiercinski's skeletal statistics, they would have disappeared millenia ago into the American gene pool if they could fade from 13.5 percent to 4.5 percent in a few brief centuries. The two major Pacific migrations of the first Americans occurred, after all, about 50,000 and 20,000 years ago, respectively, according to the most recent datings. (Some have put it as early as 70,000 years ago, others as late as 13,000. In terms of the point I am making, the fade out of any African element that came in at the very beginning of the Bering Strait migrations, the current dispute over those dates does not matter.)

Van Sertima 1986, *African Presence in Early America*, p. 65

On Dating of the First Contact
and Nature of Its Influence

The change of dating does not fundamentally affect the main proposition. It does not alter the situation in any major particular. The Egypto-Nubian ritual and technological complex was roughly the same in both periods of proposed contact. As archeologists discovered in the late seventies, it is Nubia, not Egypt, that is the creator of pharaonic civilization. No expedition under Ramses II or Ramses III (and here it should be noted again that South American cocaine has been detected in the mummy of Ramses II—see part 3 on South America) no expedition under the Ramessides would have excluded the Nubian although it would have been dominated by the Egyptian. The physical features of the two peoples in 1200 B.C. would have been the same (see 1200 B.C. painting in the frontispiece of this book). This shows the Egyptian and the Nubian, making no real distinction between the two brothers save in their positions of power in that period of time in relation to other races in the Old World—the Indo-Aryan (i.e. the European and Asiatic) and the Semitic types. Nor does it rule out a later contact. Even if, for the sake of argument, it did, the situation would be fundamentally the same. Jairazbhoy, using the 1200 B.C. date in his analysis, arrives at roughly the same ritual and technological complex as I initially did although I feel he overstates the impact of the Egyptian on the Olmec, coming close to what I have been wrongfully accused of by my dishonest critics. Jairazbhoy is a brilliant and meticulous scholar. He has devoted half of his life, as I have, to this subject. But he has a tendency to assume a cultural vacuum in America c. 1200 B.C. I do not. I have pointed out again and again that the native Americans had their own civilization but that no civilization, whether European, African, Asiatic or American, remained the same after a significant contact with outsiders. The historical record is clear. Africa certainly did not remain the same after the invasions by the Dutch, the Portuguese, the Spanish, the French, the Germans, the British, the Greeks, the Romans, the Assyrians, the Arabs. Certainly not. Yet African civilization existed many centuries before the invasions of Europe and Asia. As for European civilization, it was never the same after the Moors— the blackamoors and the tawny Moors, the Africans and the Arabs. From mathematics to medicine, to music, even to machines, Europe was affected. This has been voluminously documented (see "Golden Age of the Moor," JAC vol. 11, 1991). Africans and Arabs established four dynasties in Europe from A.D. 711 to A.D. 1492. Yet only bigots or fools would claim that Africans and Arabs were fundamentally superior because they affected the civilization of southern Europe for 700 years or that the European is a master race because he has affected the civilization of Africa for the last 500.

My friend Rafique Jairazbhoy is no racist and his choice of dating for the first contact, in the light of the most recent carbon datings, is correct, especially in view of the new evidence now emerging from the astonishing discoveries of American cocaine in the Egypt of the Rammesides by Dr. Babalanova of Ulm. I pointed to this redating of Olmec civilization (first phase) seven years ago (1991) in my address to the Smithsonian.

According to my trio of critics, frozen in negrophobic orthodoxies, only Europeans could have initiated the passage across the world's waters. Egypto-Nubians would have had to wait for Saint Christopher's blessings in order to cross the forbidden ocean. They would also have had to seek his expert advice on the following matters before setting out: That Cuba is a continent, that South America is an island, that the Caribbean Sea is the Gulf of the Ganges. They could not have got anywhere near America without that expert navigational guidance and advice. As my critics so eloquently express it, in the titling of their latest tirade of tendentious tit-tat, mimicking Leftkowitz's *Not Out of Africa*, no, no, no, the Negroes could not go, *Not Before Columbus*.

"The Mumblings of De Montellano"

Mr. Charles Touhey
Pine West Plaza Building 2
Washington Avenue Extension
Albany, New York 12205

March 31, 1992

Dear Charles,

Thank you so much for passing on the latest instalment in the "Mumblings of de Montellano." In case you are not aware of it, his letter to you provided me with another opportunity, which I have been eagerly awaiting, to set the record straight.

Point 1: Dr. de Montellano claims that an indigenous American woman is the spitting image of the colossal stone heads, that these are roughly of one type and that she is the perfect model for them all. He suggests also, by inference, that all portrait sculpture in America in the pre-Columbian era can be accounted for by this phenotype. I have prepared a series of photographs which show some of the stone heads, especially those found at Tres Zapotes, with characteristics that make such a statement patently absurd. The one with a seven-braided hairstyle is particularly worth noting since neither Bernal nor Coe nor the National Geographic have dared to publish it. It was found in 1984 in the files of the Smithsonian and returned to public scrutiny in my edition of *Nile Valley Civilizations,* after a blackout of fifty years.

Beatriz de la Fuente, in *Las Cabezas Colosales Olmecas* says of this head: "If in some moment one happened to ponder on the existence of negroes in early Mesoamerica, such a thought would surely occur after you have seen the head at Tres Zapotes (Tres Zapotes 2) the most remote in physiognomy from our indigenous ancestors. The elevated position of this personage is revealed in the headdress, from the back of which dangles seven bands which figure braids that taper off into rings and tassels."

I have also published a series of photographs of continental African types, which display the epicanthic fold to demonstrate how little de Montellano and most Americanists know about racial types in Africa. De Montellano read Bernal who claimed that "the migration [of Africans to pre-christian America] is improbable though not impossible, and *even more improbable is the combination of epicanthus fold with Negroid faces*" (see page 27 of *The Olmec World,* University of California Press, Berkeley, 1969). Neither of these gentlemen, it appears, ever went to study in Africa nor have ever read eye-witness accounts of Africans with epicanthic fold (see Evans-Pritchard and C.G. Seligman in the Sudan and the British ethnologist C.K. Meek in Northern Nigeria). Apart from that, the epicanthic fold can be acquired in nine months. My first cousins have the epicanthic fold because my uncle married a Chinese woman in Guyana with epicanthic fold. In the case of the Olmec, intermarriage between native females and newly-arrived foreign males would not be an exceptional phenomenon. It is less the exception than the rule in culture contacts.

Point 2: De Montellano claims that since C-14 datings at San Lorenzo go back to 1200 B.C. the stone heads must have been carved out around that time.

Even if the datings were as early as the era of Ramses III (c. 1200 B.C.) the figure of the Egyptian would still be predominantly Negroid and the cultural elements suggested as influences still fundamentally the same in that period (see the color photo in one of the books I edited—*Egypt Revisited* (repeated in this book)—which shows how the Egyptian saw himself circa 1200 B.C. in relation to the Nubian and other blacks of Africa). My emphasis on the 25th dynasty as the most likely of all periods for the pre-Christian contact, was explained in the 1986 anthology I edited and I made allowance in this later work for both sides of the dating equation. Jairazbhoy's emphasis on the 1200 B.C. date, unlike my own, lay in his insistence that the outsiders came in during the very first phase and "founded" Olmec civilization. I disagree with his motive for this choice of period though not with some of the meticulously researched details of his thesis. I do not believe anyone but the natives founded Olmec civilization, regardless of whether the outsiders came in the first phase (as in the Jairazbhoy model) or in the later phase of the dating equation (as in the 1977 Van Sertima model). The evidence certainly suggests the influence of outsiders (see my Smithsonian address on the extraordinary ritual parallels between the Olmec and Egyptian). But while one may argue for an influence and in such an argument an apparent identity is put forward, only some of them will pass the acid test. But I have never claimed that the Egyptians or the Egypto-Nubians created Olmec civilization.

Nor have I claimed, as the mendacious de Montellano has claimed, that they gave the Mexicans their calendar. I made passing reference to a calendar described by a priest—the Abbé Hervas—that he pointed out had gone out of use well before Spanish times and was far removed from the Aztec calendar we found in the European contact period. Mexico was not always, as Cortez found it, a fairly centralised state. We found the peoples speaking fourteen languages. It is not impossible for them to have had more than one time-keeping model simultaneously in vastly diverse provinces centuries before the coming of the Conquistadors. The Egyptians themselves had more than one. The Stele of Canopus shows this. Dr. de Montellano, picking on me for mentioning a defunct calendar observed by the Abbé Hervas, claimed that I said the Mexican calendar was the same as the Egyptian. This is a naked and nasty lie. The Aztec 52-year cycle (which I discuss in chapter 5 of my book) bears absolutely no resemblance to any Egyptian timekeeping model. Its indigenous and unique nature would be obvious even to an idiot. The statement made by Abbé Hervas on a defunct calendar in a part of pre-Spanish America, which he claimed conformed with an earlier Egyptian model, was deliberately cited out of context to make me appear like a facile diffusionist. *De Montellano knows this!!*

Point 3: He is not only interested, however, in a debate on the question of pre-Columbian contacts. He is intent on misrepresenting my position on the matter of race in order to slander me. He claims, for example, that I think *native Americans were too stupid to create their own civilization and it required diffusion from superior black people.* This is not based on anything I said but pure personal venom. It misrepresents everything that I am, everything that I have said, everything that I have done.

Let me quote from statements I have made about the native American both in *They Came Before Columbus* (1976) in *African Presence in Early America* (1986) and in my *Testimony to a Congressional subcommittee* overseeing the work of the Christopher Columbus Quincentenary Commission (July 7, 1987).

a. "I think it is necessary to make this clear—since partisan and ethnocentric scholarship is the order of the day—that the emergence of the "Negroid" face, which the archaeological (i.e. skeletal and iconographic and cultural) data overwhelmingly confirms, in no way presupposes the lack of a native originality . . . *"They Came Before Columbus,* p. 147.

b. "By the time any outsiders came in any significant numbers, the Olmec would already have had some kind of home-grown civilization. A priest-caste would have emerged, an elite group that governed the rural villages and started to put a stamp, a distinctive stamp, upon the culture, like the jaguar motif, for example. This motif is already in evidence in the 1200 B.C. find at Copalillo (by my colleague at Rutgers, Dr. Hammond). I have never argued that this was brought to America by outsiders. Whatever the arguments of some of my colleagues, and I say this with the deepest respect, they are too apt to assume a native vacuum in pre-Christian America . . . I cannot subscribe to the notion that civilization suddenly dropped onto the American earth from the Egyptian heaven." *African Presence in Early America,* page 16.

c. "Although it is fashionable to make a special case for one's racial or national identity, I want to point out that I am a cosmopolis of almost all old world and new world races. I am therefore concerned that our vision of the world, of these Americas, take full cognizance of all these peoples and all these ancestors so that one does not live in constant war and uneasiness with the other.

"The European side of me is insulting the Native American side of me by calling these voyages "voyages of discovery", also insulting the African side of me by insisting that these voyages to America were the first, when there is so much evidence to suggest that the Atlantic coastal peoples (the African) made significant contact with the American long before the era of Columbus.

"I came here before you to correct this myth, to present a more objective vision of our plural American legacy."

—Van Sertima before Congress
(July 7, 1989)

This man has read everything I have officially written on this subject. Whatever his disagreement with my views, he knows full well that I am no racist. He knows full well that I have edited a dozen anthologies, displaying the best essays on African civilization history not only by African-American and Caribbean but European, Jewish,

African and European-American scholars. He must know that I am beyond racist thinking, having come from a family that has married into every major race of the world. As I intimated before and let me spell it out now in personal detail—my uncle, Alick Van Sertima married a Chinese woman and my first cousins—Sheila Van Sertima (London) and Anita (New York)—have the epicanthic fold which he argues cannot appear on Africans living among native Americans of Mongolian cast of feature. The epicanthic fold on the eyes of my cousins was acquired in nine months.

Also, art styles, even when responsive to novel facets of alien physiognomy, do not always abandon every aspect of their earlier formalization of faces. Thus Nefertiti (who is daughter of the Persian king Dushratta) is represented with the striking prognathism and full-lipped features of her Afro-Egyptian husband, Akhnaton, and their two very African-looking daughters. We are practically looking at his feminine twin in the Temple of Nefertiti. Yet the Berlin bust shows clearly she is no African. Again, the bust of Buddha is presented by the Greeks in an art style so formalized that, were it not for the labelling of the sculpture, we would certainly pronounce him European.

The stone heads do not stand by themselves. As Andrez Wiercinski and A. Vargas Guadarrama have shown, the craniological and skeletal evidence corroborates the Africoid presence suggested by some of these heads. I can go on for days on this matter, Charles, but I must close now. It is a pity one has to waste so much time to deal with the venom and malice of this little man with the big name. As you know, he is a professor of anthropology at Wayne State University in Michigan. He also pretends to comment with authority on the *guanin* complex of words and their linguistic identities in the Caribbean and some parts of Mexico when he knows absolutely nothing about African languages. But I am grateful to him in a way. He has made such a notorious celebrity of me in Michigan that a book chain there has just ordered 3000 copies of my book for the schools. I think you will enjoy my comment on this gentleman and his intellectual pretensions in note 6 of my address to the Smithsonian which is to be published by the Smithsonian Press in 1994.

Please keep me informed of his future underhand attacks on my reputation since he circulates these letters surreptitiously in many places.

—Ivan Van Sertima

More on "The Mumblings of De Montellano"

Bernard Ortiz de Montellano, professor of anthropology, Wayne State University, Detroit, Michigan, is the author of a pamphlet circulating privately in many schools, the first version of which places in quotation marks things that I never said. Where I show that the Olmec is a homegrown civilization and that I am not speaking of its origin or its major source of inspiration but presenting evidence that indicates an outside influence, de Montellano insists that I am arguing that the Olmec stone heads are all African and Olmec culture and technology are African. De Montellano also claims that all the stone and terracotta heads found among the Olmec are "spitting images of the native," even the Tres Zapotes head with seven braids, which a reputable expert on the matter, Beatrice de la Fuente, claims is "the most remote in physiognomy from our indigenous ancestors." Though trained as a linguist, he contends that the "guanin" complex of words for gold found in West African Sarakole, Soninke, Gadsago, Vai, Mende, Kissi, Kono, Peul, Mandinka, Dyula, Malinke, Khassoke, and Bambara were native to the Americas (while frankly admitting that he knows absolutely nothing about African languages) and when interconnected plant terms are cited from specific areas in South America for their startling identities with West African words for the plant found in pre-Columbian South American graves, he blandly ignores these, such as the African *bakoko* for a banana imported from Asia to Africa in the twelfth century, appearing in South American languages.

While it has been made clear to him that I have distanced myself from a lot of Wiener's linguistics, he contends that if I do not dismiss all of it, my thesis is just a repeat of this pioneer's early probings. De Montellano refuses to consider the work done since Wiener, as though scholarship in this area has stood still since the 1920s. He deliberately ignores recent studies done on skeletons by Wiercinski and Guadarrama; on the excavation of pre-Columbian terra-cotta (Von Wuthenau 1969);

on plants and currents and Atlantic crossings with pre-Christian African vessels, as related by Hannes Lindemann, Alain Bombard, and Thor Heyerdahl; and on preparations for medieval expeditions reported by Masalik el Absar fir Mamalik el Amsar and al-Qalqashandi in both Mali court traditions and Arabic documents. He also ignores the metallurgical and cartographic evidence (especially the Piri Re'is map) and the eyewitness reports by Europeans, including Columbus, entering the New World for the first time.

De Montellano also claims that I said the Mexicans got their calendar from the Egyptians, which is an outright falsehood, since I point to the existence of four calendars in America and merely report the claim made by the Abbé Hervas to Clavigero that one of these is in conformity with an Egyptian calendar. De Montellano argues that America, alone among world civilizations, was a virginal entity and that if anyone were to claim that Native Americans were influenced by anyone outside of the post-Columbian European, such a person would be trying to downgrade the Native American people in order to upgrade his own ethnic community. He is ignorant, of course, as he is in most matters, of the fact that my ethnic identity and community is as much Native American (Macusi Indian) as African.

From my Smithsonian address, 1991

Concerning the False Accusation that I Claimed Africans Founded the First American Civilization

At this point I wish to clear up a misconception or rather to expose a scandalous misrepresentation of my position. I have not claimed—and resent being accused of having claimed—that Africans founded the first significant American civilization. I have never said so. Aboriginal or Native Americans were here for thousands of years. How could migrants crossing the oceans, save those who came later in a massive movement of millions, *totally* alter the face of their civilization? Rather, I pointed to specific influences that the evidence seemed to suggest. Alien groups, however small, migrants from outside, can have a significant impact on a native civilization. This is true of all the world's civilizations: whether they be African, Asian, or European, they will be affected by other civilizations. That is the very nature of civilization. The only people who are not easily affected are primitives. They live in an impervious glass bubble, most of them. That is why they remain fairly static for thousands of years. Richness, variety, and complexity arise when civilizations reach out and draw things into their systems. They take the other, the alien, the new. They transform it. They make it their own. They have their own "thing," but they draw incessantly from others. This is natural. It has nothing to do with cultural inferiority or superiority. Let me make it utterly clear. I am not trying to build some new model of African superiority.

Smithsonian Address 1991

An Appeal for Change in Our
Methodologies and Approaches

If we want to get the essence of Europe, the grandeur of Europe, the technological ingenuity of Europe, we go to the sophisticated centers. But we ignored the centers of Africa. It was not only because of prejudice. We could not study it easily. It was a shattered world and that is one of the things I want to make clear from the beginning. You cannot study America and you cannot study Africa the way you study Europe. Europe has, in spite of its many wars, what I would like to call "an archival continuity." Africa does not. America does not. There were three systematic and deliberate destructions of documents in this country. Bishop de Landa in the Yucatan said, "Burn them all. They are works of the Devil." That is why it has become necessary to adopt what some people like to call an "ahistorical" method. It is, in fact, the only possible historical method for dealing with such shattered worlds. You can't just go into the little books that we think are complete and study what happened in early America. You have to go to botany and linguistics and oceanography and into studies of crania and pottery and even cartography in order to find the missing pieces of these shattered worlds.

This time, this place, is no longer the America we are examining, the America we are debating. Look around this room. There is probably no native American in this room. You could go to parts of Africa, too, like Cairo, and you stand in a room lecturing and there are almost no indigenous Egyptians. An awesome catastrophe has befallen these broken worlds. And one is not saying this out of protest. One is just making clear a historical reality that we have to come to terms with. To do so we have to change our methodologies, our approaches

From address to the Smithsonian
November, 1991

History as a Guide to Modern Political Action

I conclude this address, ladies and gentlemen, with both an inspirational note and a salutary warning. We are on the brink of great change in this country as well as great danger. Nothing major should be done, nothing major attempted, without great thought, without great caution. We should drink deep from the well of our history but in a way that nourishes rather than simply titillates us, poisons us, or divides us. History is a critical complement to contemporary reality and it is particularly helpful to those who have lost their way in the world because the footprints of their past have vanished or been erased. But let not history stand like the ghostly twinkle of a long dead star on the horizon of our consciousness. It should be a dynamic beam of light in daily motion across the sky of our minds. It should charge us not only with a surge of new pride but the electric energy of creative action. For it to animate us thus, it will demand, it will most certainly demand, a corresponding animation of consciousness. History is a window through which we see only half of ourselves. The other half may be quickened into life by the image of the twin we see looking back through the window. Let us, however, never fool ourselves that there, in the mirror of time, we can see our totality and therefore know not only where we have been and what we have done but also what we must do now to get where we think we are going.

History does not provide, and should not be seen as providing, save in a few isolated instances, a tried and tested program of action for contemporary situations. What may have worked in 2000 B.C. may lead to disaster in A.D. 2000. What failed in 2000 B.C. might work marvels in A.D. 2000. We learn the lessons of the past to alert us to a range of human situations and sometimes to mistakes which we would otherwise have to repeat ourselves in order to learn from them. History enables us, therefore, to act with greater caution and wisdom in the future. But we must constantly and simultaneously be aware of the many new variables that have entered the world. The emotional infantilism which still divides and imprisons man, his racial or tribal antagonisms, may not have changed very much but the world we live in has changed. It is no longer a neat conglomerate of separate and sovereign entities. What happens in Bosnia is not just between Muslims, the Croats, and the Serbs, what happens in Haiti is not just between Aristide and the junta of General Raoul Cedras, what happens in Rwanda is not just between the Tutsi and the Hutu, what happened in Chernobyl was not just a Russian disaster. Our modern world is intimately intersected and connected. We are living in the same global house. The voice of my most distant neighbor is just a radiowave or light-wave away.

Contemporary reality calls for an updated program, therefore, a subtletisation of liberation strategies. Consciousness of history is a critical part of this. Relating it to the complexities of the modern world is equally critical. We cannot say, as we have done, with an earlier and understandable innocence, that when we know what we have done wrong in the distant past we can make sure we shall not do it again. For what may have been dead wrong 500 years ago may be a workable strategy in our time. What we can learn from history, however, is to have, through a more total vision of our past, a truer and more total sense of ourselves, a better ground upon which to build our lives, a more informed and illuminated base upon which to make decisions about the role we should play in our family, our community, our country and the world. Too many people believe that the emotional boost this new history can bring to some of us will be enough. It will not be.

The vision of our former stature in the world must penetrate our consciousness so deeply that it begins to transform the degrading and dwarf-like habits of our present thought and action, habits which have crippled our progress for too long. This heightened awareness of the best in our past can stimulate and inspire and heal us but it must blend intelligently with a maturing vision of the living present if it is to be of practical value. Unless the two dimensions—the past and the present—are fused creatively, we shall dance forever to the tune of slogans, we shall be titillated by the vulgar drama of history rather than be galvanized into new thought and action by the current of lightning, the current of insights, springing from the past. . . .

From Address to the National Council of Black Studies—Republic of Guyana, South America—June 4, 1994

Biography

Ivan Van Sertima was born in Guyana, South America. He was educated at the School of Oriental and African Studies (London University) and the Rutgers Graduate School and holds degrees in African Studies and Anthropology. From 1957–1959 he served as a Press and Broadcasting Officer in the Guyana Information Services. During the decade of the 1960s he broadcast weekly from Britain to Africa and the Caribbean.

He is a literary critic, a linguist, and an anthropologist and has made a name in all three fields.

As a literary critic, he is the author of *Caribbean Writers,* a collection of critical essays on the Caribbean novel. He is also the author of several major literary reviews published in Denmark, India, Britain and the United States. He was honored for his work in this field by being asked by the Nobel Committee of the Swedish Academy to nominate candidates for the Nobel Prize in Literature from 1976–1980. He has also been honored as an historian of world repute by being asked to join UNESCO's *International Commission for Rewriting the Scientific and Cultural History of Mankind.*

As a linguist, he has published essays on the dialect of the Sea Islands off the Georgia Coast. He is also the compiler of the *Swahili Dictionary of Legal Terms,* based on his field work in Tanzania, East Africa, in 1967.

He is the author of *They Came Before Columbus: The African Presence in Ancient America,* which was published by Random House in 1977 and is now in its twenty-first printing. It was published in French in 1981 and in the same year was awarded the Clarence L.

Holte Prize, a prize awarded every two years "for a work of excellence in literature and the humanities relating to the cultural heritage of Africa and the African diaspora."

Professor of African Studies at Rutgers University, Van Sertima was also Visiting Professor at Princeton University. He is the Editor of the *Journal of African Civilizations,* which he founded in 1979 and has published several major anthologies which have influenced the development of a new multicultural curriculum in the U.S. These anthologies include *Blacks in Science: Ancient and Modern, Black Women in Antiquity, Egypt Revisited, Egypt: Child of Africa, Nile Valley Civilizations, African Presence in the Art of the Americas, African Presence in Early Asia* (co-edited with Runoko Rashidi), *African Presence in Early Europe, African Presence in Early America, Great African Thinkers* (co-edited with Larry Williams), *Great Black Leaders: Ancient and Modern* and *Golden Age of the Moor.*

Professor Van Sertima has lectured at more than 100 universities in the United States and has also lectured in Canada, the Caribbean, South America and Europe. He defended his highly controversial thesis on the African presence in pre-Columbian America before the Smithsonian which published his address in 1995. He also appeared before a Congressional Committee on July 7, 1987 to challenge the Columbus myth.

Jacqueline L. Patten-Van Sertima has been a photographer for over 24 years, expanding her expertise in this field by not only maintaining the title of photographic consultant and art director, but by designing book covers for all issues of the renowned publication, the *Journal of African Civilizations,* for the past 14 years.

She is best known, however, for her significant contribution to social awareness through photography. Her fine technique of hand-painted black and white photography was developed in an effort to more deeply explore the subject matter of the image, the visual statement being made, rather than become preoccupied with the superficial glare and glamour of color. Her light touch enhances and brings into more sensitive reality the mental impression of the image. Predominantly, her subject matter deals with positive images of people of African descent.

Her photographic exhibitions include: The Museum of the City of New York, the National Urban League, Columbia University, Washington Square East Galleries of New York University, the Ziegfield Gallery, Lincoln Center, Hunter College Arts Gallery, Rockland State College, the New Muse Museum, Womanart Galleries, ACBAW Center for the Arts, the Benin Gallery, Brockman Gallery and various banks throughout the country. She was also interviewed and exhibited on television's *For You Black Woman* (1979).

Ms. Patten-Van Sertima has won international distinction for her hand-painted photography, its excellent execution, as well as for its sociological significance through a variety of publications. Listed in the Cambridge *International Who's Who of Women, Who's Who of Intellectuals, International Register of Profiles, Who's Who in the East, International Who's Who in the World, Directory of Distinguished Americans, Community Leaders of the World* and *Personalities of America* for "outstanding artistic achievement and contributions to society" (1983–present).

Her awards include: American Visions, Lincoln Center's seventh annual awards exhibition, Foundation for the Community of Artists Target Presentations award, first prize in Mademoiselle's fourteenth annual photography competition and Lincoln Center's photography award presented by Womanart Galleries.

Publications include: *The Black Photographers Annual* and *Black Photographers: An Illustrated Bio-Bibliography 1940-1987* sponsored by the Schomberg Center for Research in Black Culture.

Ms. Patten-Van Sertima received her B.S. in Psychology and M.S. in Education from Hunter College, New York.

A Listener's Library of Educational Classics

Legacies, Inc., the audio arm of the *Journal of African Civilizations,* was established by Mrs. Jacqueline L. Patten-Van Sertima in answer to a genuine need and many requests from parents and teachers across the country. They needed a widespread, easily accessible and responsible medium of communication. It not only had to serve as a learning tool, but as an informational vehicle for educational strategies that hold promise for our youths. They also needed a dynamic and expedient way to absorb and disseminate information as well as a bridge to parents whose time for relearning and participation in the educational process was limited. So, in keeping with the highly controversial needs of the times, Legacies, Inc., was born.

In most of our audio cassette tapes, you will be hearing the voice of Dr. Ivan Van Sertima, founder and editor of the *Journal of African Civilizations.* His untiring fervor has made learning for everyone an exciting adventure through time. The lectures, by a variety of speakers, are brilliant, stimulating, passionate and absorbing. It is the drama of forgotten peoples and civilizations, brought to you through an unusually fresh and liberating vision of the human legacy.

AUDIO TAPES

__African Presence in Early America and Address to the Smithsonian	$10.00
__African Presence in Early Asia—R. Rashidi and Van Sertima	$10.00
__African Presence in Early Europe	$10.00
__African Presence in World Cultures (excerpts from all tapes—120 mins.)	$11.00
__The Black Family—J.H. Clarke and Van Sertima	$10.00
__Black Women in Antiquity	$10.00
__Blacks in Science: ancient and modern	$10.00
__Early America Revisited	$11.00
__Egypt: Child of Africa	$10.00
__Egypt Revisited	$10.00
__Golden Age of the Moor—R. Rashidi and Van Sertima	$10.00
__Great African Thinkers—C.A. Diop	$10.00
__Great Black Leaders: ancient and modern	$10.00
__The Legacy of Columbus—Jan Carew	$10.00
__Re-Educating Our Children	$10.00
__Socialization of the African Child—Asa G. Hilliard	$10.00
__They Came Before Columbus	$10.00
__Van Sertima Before Congress	$10.00

Date _____

Name _____

Address _____

City/State _____

Zip _____ Tel. No. _____

Check and money orders should be made payable to:

"Legacies"

Jacqueline L. Patten-Van Sertima
347 Felton Ave.
Highland Park, New Jersey 08904

Please include postage:

1 tape 1.00
2 tapes 1.70
3 tapes 2.15
4-10 tapes 3.00
11-18 tapes 4.50

Please Note: *Tapes cannot be purchased through bookstores or other vendors.*

A Series of Historical Classics

The *Journal of African Civilizations,* founded in 1979, has gained a reputation for excellence and uniqueness among historical and anthropological journals. It is recognized as a valuable information source for both the layman and student. It has created a different historical perspective within which to view the ancestor of the African-American and the achievement and potential of black people the world over.

It is the only historical journal in the English-speaking world which focuses on the heartland rather than on the periphery of African civilization. It therefore removes the "primitive" from the center stage it has occupied in Eurocentric histories and anthropologies of the African. The *Journal of African Civilizations* is dedicated to the celebration of black genius, to a revision of the role of the African in the world's great civilizations, the contribution of Africa to the achievement of man in the arts and sciences. It emphasizes what blacks have given to the world, not what they have lost.

BOOKS

Add $7.50 per book foreign airmail.

__African Presence in Early America $15.00
__African Presence in Early Asia $20.00
(out of print until May)
__African Presence in Early Europe $20.00
__Black Women in Antiquity $20.00
__Blacks in Science: Ancient and Modern $20.00
*Early America Revisited $20.00
__Egypt Revisited $20.00
__Egypt: Child of Africa $20.00
__Golden Age of the Moor $20.00
__Great African Thinkers—C.A. Diop $20.00
(out of print until June)
__Great Black Leaders: Ancient and Modern $20.00
__Nile Valley Civilizations (cancelled)

Postage for above books:
$1.75 per order of single book.
.75 more for each additional book.

*Early America Revisited $20.00
(*For this particular book, please make checks*   postage $ 1.75
payable to "Ivan Van Sertima")

Date _____

Name _____
Address _____
City/State _____
Zip _____ Tel. No. _____

Check and money orders for all books above (except *Early America Revisited*) should be made payable to:

"Journal of African Civilizations"

Ivan Van Sertima (Editor)
Journal of African Civilizations
Africana Studies Department
Beck Hall
Rutgers University
New Brunswick, New Jersey 08903

Orders for *Early America Revisited* should be made payable to "Ivan Van Sertima".

Copies of this book may be ordered from:

Dr. Ivan Van Sertima
Africana Studies Department
Beck Hall
Rutgers University
New Brunswick, NJ 08903

NOTES